University of Miami
Coral Gables, Florida

Written by Shawn Wines
Edited by Julie Wesolowski

*Additional contributions by Adam Burns, Omid Gohari,
Christina Koshzow, Chris Mason, Joey Rahimi,
Jon Skindzier, Luke Skurman*

ISBN # 1-59658-162-X
ISSN # 1552-1397
© Copyright 2005 CollegeProwler
All Rights Reserved
Printed in the U.S.A.
www.collegeprowler.com

Special thanks to Babs Carryer, Andy Hannah, LaunchCyte, Tim O'Brien, Bob Sehlinger, Thomas Emerson, Andrew Skurman, Barbara Skurman, Bert Mann, Dave Lehman, Daniel Fayock, Chris Babyak,The Donald H. Jones Center for Entrepreneurship, Terry Slease, Jerry McGinnis, Bill Ecenberger, Idie McGinty, Kyle Russell, Jacque Zaremba, Larry Winderbaum, Paul Kelly, Roland Allen, Jon Reider, Team Evankovich, Julie Fenstermaker, Lauren Varacalli, Abu Noaman, Jason Putorti, Mark Exler, Daniel Steinmeyer, Jared Cohon, Gabriela Oates, Tri Ad Litho, David Koegler, and Glen Meakem

Bounce Back Team: John Harper and Harry Madhanagopal

College Prowler™
5001 Baum Blvd.
Suite 456
Pittsburgh, PA 15213

Phone: (412) 697-1390, 1(800) 290-2682
Fax: (412) 697-1396, 1(800) 772-4972
E-mail: info@collegeprowler.com
Website: www.collegeprowler.com

Welcome to College Prowler™

During the writing of College Prowler's guidebooks, we felt it was critical that our content was unbiased and unaffiliated with any college or university. We think it's important that our readers get honest information and a realistic impression of the student opinions on any campus — that's why if any aspect of a particular school is terrible, we (unlike a campus brochure) intend to publish it. While we do keep an eye out for the occasional extremist — the cheerleader or the cynic — we take pride in letting the students tell it like it is. We strive to create a book that's as representative as possible of each particular campus. Our books cover both the good and the bad, and whether the survey responses point to recurring trends or a variation in opinion, these sentiments are directly and proportionally expressed through our guides.

College Prowler guidebooks are in the hands of students throughout the entire process of their creation. Because you can't make student-written guides without the students, we have students at each campus who help write, randomly survey their peers, edit, layout, and perform accuracy checks on every book that we publish. From the very beginning, student writers gather the most up-to-date stats, facts, and inside information on their colleges. They fill each section with student quotes and summarize the findings in editorial reviews. In addition, each school receives a collection of letter grades (A through F) that reflect student opinion and help to represent contentment, prominence, or satisfaction for each of our 20 specific categories. Just as in grade school, the higher the mark the more content, more prominent, or more satisfied the students are with the particular category.

Once a book is written, additional students serve as editors and check for accuracy even more extensively. Our bounce-back team — a group of randomly selected students who have no involvement with the project — are asked to read over the material in order to help ensure that the book accurately expresses every aspect of the university and its students. This same process is applied to the 200-plus schools College Prowler currently covers. Each book is the result of endless student contributions, hundreds of pages of research and writing, and countless hours of hard work. All of this has led to the creation of a student information network that stretches across the nation to every school that we cover. It's no easy accomplishment, but it's the reason that our guides are such a great resource.

When reading our books and looking at our grades, keep in mind that every college is different and that the students who make up each school are not uniform — as a result, it is important to assess schools on a case-by-case basis. Because it's impossible to summarize an entire school with a single number or description, each book provides a dialogue, not a decision, that's made up of 20 different topics and hundreds of student quotes. In the end, we hope that this guide will serve as a valuable tool in your college selection process. Enjoy!

OMID GOHARI ◯ CHRISTINA KOSHZOW ◯ CHRIS MASON ◯ JOEY RAHIMI ◯ LUKE SKURMAN ◯
Founders of College Prowler™

Table of Contents

Introduction from the Author

Growing up in South Florida, I had the same impression as most people about the University of Miami. In the early 90's, it had a reputation for being a party school with a bunch of cheaters on its football team. Ten years later, when I decided to come to UM, my thoughts had changed. The academics at this school have been steadily improving since the 70's, back when it was known to beach-loving hippies as "Suntan U." Our football team is great once again, and the old charges of recruiting violations and paying players are gone.

The thing that surprised me the most after my first few days here was the beauty of the campus. It's obvious why we're usually listed among the nicest college campuses in the nation, although it's sad to see students ignoring their beautiful surroundings and complaining about little things like the Taco Bell in the food court only having express items (no Mexican Pizzas!?!). The bodies seen around campus are absolutely stunning, but students usually complain that their peers are shallow and only interested in looks. Maybe these are just bitter words from lonely students, but it does seem difficult to meet people sometimes if you don't look like a model. Still, there are plenty of normal people that are perfectly happy here.

Judging from the attitudes of most students, this complaint seems to be one of only a few. People complain about little things like the heat or the difficulty of their physics classes, but most students appear to be really happy at UM. For one, UM is a great place to tell people you go to school. Because of our great sports history, everyone knows what UM is. Not to mention, it's very satisfying to read away messages from friends at other schools about how many feet of snow they're trudging through to get to class while you're in shorts and sandals.

The facilities on campus are certainly a highlight, ranging from the new, state-of-the-art Wellness Center to the movie theater and basketball arena. At the center of campus is a beautiful lake, which students walk by daily on the way to and from class. On the shore of the lake is the student union, called the UC, which houses restaurants, lounges, and a bookstore.

Staying true to its Miami home, UM also features a swimming pool and a bar on campus. But the most fun you'll have if you come here will be off campus, at the bars and shops of Coconut Grove or the clubs and trendy nightspots in South Beach.

Before deciding on a college, you should ask yourself what you want to do for the next four years. If you're looking for a quiet school with a focus on studying and academics, you may not be happy here. That isn't to say that you'd hate it, but the stereotype of Miami being a party spot with great weather and gorgeous people, although shortsighted, is not entirely false.

Shawn Wines, Author
University of Miami

By the Numbers

General Information

University of Miami
Coral Gables, FL 33146

Control:
Private

Academic Calendar:
Semester

Religious Affiliation:
None

Founded:
1925

Website:
www.miami.edu

Main Phone:
(305) 284-2211

Admissions Phone:
(305) 284-4323

Student Body

**Full-Time
Undergraduates:**
9,184

**Part-Time
Undergraduates:**
812

**Total Male
Undergraduates:**
4,187

**Total Female
Undergraduates:**
5,809

Male to Female Ratio:
58.1% to 41.9

Admissions

Overall Acceptance Rate:
44%

Early Decision Acceptance Rate:
37%

Regular Acceptance Rate:
63%

Total Applicants:
16,851

Total Acceptances:
7,490

Freshman Enrollment:
2,078

Yield (% of admitted students who actually enroll):
27.7%

Transfer Applications Received:
2,454

Transfer Applications Accepted:
1,216

Transfer Students Enrolled:
575

Transfer Applicant Acceptance Rate:
50%

Early Decision Available?
Yes

Early Action Available?
Yes

Early Decision Deadline:
November 1

Early Decision Notification:
December 15

Regular Decision Deadline:
February 1

Regular Decision Notification:
April 15

Must-Reply-By Date:
May 1

Common Application Accepted?
Yes

Supplemental Forms?
Yes

Admissions Phone:
(305) 284-4323

Admissions E-mail:
admission@miami.edu

Admissions Website:
http://www.miami.edu/admission

SAT I or ACT Required?
Either

SAT I Range (25th – 75th Percentile):
1120 – 1340

SAT I Verbal Range (25th – 75th Percentile):
550 – 660

SAT I Math Range (25th – 75th Percentile):
570-680

Retention Rate:
87%

**Top 10% of
High School Class:**
60%

Application Fee:
$55

**SAT II Requirements for
Honors Program in Medicine**:

For all applicants, English
(with or without writing),
Physics, Chemistry or Biology,
and Math are required.

Financial Information

Full-Time Tuition:
$27,840 per year

Part-Time Tuition:
$845 per credit
(most classes are 3 credits)

$40 registration fee
per semester

Room and Board:
$8,602

Books and Supplies for class:
$808 per year

**Average Need-Based
Financial Aid Package:**
$22,940
(including loans, work-study,
grants, and other sources)

**Students Who
Applied For Financial Aid:**
62%

Students Who Received Aid:
55%

Financial Aid Forms Deadline:
February 15

Financial Aid Phone:
(305) 284-5212

Financial Aid E-mail:
ofas@miami.edu

Financial Aid Website:
http://www.miami.edu/ofas

Academics

The Lowdown On...
Academics

Degrees Awarded:
Bachelor
Master
Doctorate

Most Popular Areas of Study:
23% business
12% visual/performing arts
10% biology
10% communication and
     journalism
8% social sciences

Undergraduate Schools:
Architecture
Arts and Sciences
Business
Communication
Education
Engineering
Music
Nursing

Full-Time Faculty:	**4 Year Graduation Rate %:**
2,152	53%

Faculty with Terminal Degree:
96%

5 Year Graduation Rate %:
65%

Student-to-Faculty Ratio:

13:1

6 Year Graduation Rate %:
67%

Average Course Load:
Not Available

Special Degree Options
Dual Degree Honors Programs: Biomedical Engineering, Marine Geology, Physical Therapy, Medicine, Latin American Studies
Honors Program in Medicine (Six-Year Accelerated Bachelor of Science and Doctorate of Medicine)

AP Test Score Requirements
Possible credit for scores of 3, 4, or 5 depending on specific requirements of the program

IB Test Score Requirements
Possible credit for scores of 4, 5, 6, or 7

Sample Academic Clubs
Florida Engineering Society, Filmmakers' Association, German Club, Honors Student Association, National Broadcasting Society, School of Architecture Student Council

Did You Know?

 Feel trapped in your dorm room? Many students, equipped with wireless Internet on their laptops, head outside to **study by the lake** or under a tree.

• At the end of every semester, students receive surveys asking them to **rank each of their professors** in various categories. The results are tallied and posted on the school network to help students select their courses.

• Teaching assistants are **rare in most courses** at UM. Even freshmen lecture classes are almost always taught by full-time faculty members.

Best Places to Study

Library, Dorm Study Lounges, University Center, Outside

Students Speak Out On...
Academics

"The teachers vary by department. Teachers in the math and science departments rarely speak English fluently, which hinders the learning capability of the students. For the most part however, the material covered in classes is intriguing. That is, when you can comprehend what is being taught."

"**Most of the teachers are extremely well prepared** about the classes they are teaching. Only one teacher I've had really has not been geared for UM because of his teaching methods. The classes have been very interesting throughout the years and I feel that I have learned a lot."

"**My teachers are all very friendly and willing to help out their students.** They try their best to make each class interesting, and they stay up-to-date on current trends in society, allowing them to relate to each student."

"My teachers have made each class challenging while also making them fun by adding jokes into their lectures and having a surprise from time to time. I would say that **I have had a positive experience with all of my teachers.**"

"The teachers at UM are for the most part pretty cool. There are, of course, some that are better than the others. I find that **all the teachers are accessible** and that is a positive. They are also more than willing to help with any questions."

Q "The teachers here are very friendly, but you can make them into whatever you want. If you want a friend, that's an option, and so is being the person in the back of the room, learning in your own quiet way. Either way, they will stimulate your mind. Most classes are very interesting, and **some professors are very entertaining in their teaching methods.**"

Q "**Some classes are interesting but it really depends on the subject.** For example, math classes are boring to me, whereas the science classes are interesting. It really depends on what you prefer as a person."

Q "**The teachers are willing to spend a lot of time with you personally**, maybe because this is a private school. Classes are interesting once you get past the intro level if you're doing something you like, but they're pretty good about AP credits here, so it's easy to AP-out of intro level courses."

Q "The teachers range from very passionate to extremely boring, but this is the case with every school. In general, **most classes are interesting. It really depends on the teacher and subject** (it's hard to make math interesting to most people)."

Q "**My teachers are great.** They offer me a lot of advice and always have time for me. Most of my classes are interesting."

The College Prowler Take On...
Academics

Back in the 1970's, the University of Miami was known as Suntan U. Fun loving hippies flocked from around the country to party on their parents' money for four years. Since that era ended, UM has done a great job in climbing its way into the top tier of American colleges. Although Miami is still a great party town, most of UM's students are here with academics in mind as well as nightlife and beaches. As a school becomes more prestigious, it builds a strong faculty, and that's exactly what UM has done. Students seem to like their professors, even if they complain regularly about homework and exams. Although complaints about the amount of work and grading are common, it's rare to hear anyone claim that a professor does not know the subject he's teaching.

It's not hard to see that UM is never going to be one of the strongest colleges in the country academically. Harvard, Princeton, and Yale don't need to worry about losing professors to UM, unless they really hate the New England cold. But Miami is building a great university by combining academics with other aspects of college life. It's safe to say, then, that while academics are not hurting UM, they're not the best thing about it. The professors are mostly good, and there are a few great ones, but overall it feels like a place that's going to teach you what books say you need to know, not necessarily what you actually want to know.

B

The College Prowler™ Grade on
Academics: B

A high Academics grade generally indicates that professors are knowledgeable, accessible, and genuinely interested in their students' welfare. Other determining factors include class size, how well professors communicate, and whether or not classes are engaging.

Local Atmosphere

The Lowdown On...
Local Atmosphere

Region:
Southeast

City, State:
Coral Gables, FL

Setting:
Coastal

Distance from Orlando:
3.5 hours

Distance from Key West:
3.5 hours

→

Points of Interest:

South Beach
Coconut Grove
Sunset Place
Florida Keys
Everglades
Lowe Art Museum
American Airlines Arena
Bayside
Pro Player Stadium
Vizcaya Mansion
Miami Jai Alai
Little Havana
Venetian Pool
Metro Zoo

Closest Shopping Malls or Plazas:

Sunset Place
Dadeland Mall
Cocowalk
The Falls
Village of Merrick Park

Closest Movie Theatres:

Bill Cosford Cinema
Memorial Building, University of Miami
Phone: (305) 284-4861

AMC Sunset Place 24
5701 Sunset Dr., South Miami
Phone: (305) 466-0450

AMC Cocowalk 16
3015 Grand Ave., Coconut Grove
Phone: (305) 466-0450

Major Sports Teams:

Dolphins (football)
Marlins (baseball)
Heat (basketball)
Panthers (hockey)

City Websites

http://ci.miami.fl.us
http://miami.citysearch.com
http://www.digitalcity.com/southflorida

Did You Know?
5 Fun Facts about Miami:

- One of Miami's most notable and fun places is its large Cuban neighborhood, known as **Little Havana**. Head to Calle Ocho (8th Street) to try some great Cuban food and sample other aspects of a fascinating culture.

- Miami's trendy nightlife crowd makes South Beach a hot spot on any night of the week. **Keep an eye out for celebrities on the weekends**, when the clubs get invaded by stars like Will Smith, P. Diddy, and Jennifer Lopez

- An hour drive south will take you to the start of the Florida Keys, **a string of beautiful islands** that ends at one of the area's most popular party spots, Key West.

- You never know who you might see walking the streets of Miami. The city was home to at least four recent blockbuster films: Bad Boys II, 2 Fast 2 Furious, Stuck on You, and Out of Time. **Countless other music videos and commercials were shot in Miami**, as well as films like Scarface and The Birdcage.

- **Having a car in college is a great luxury**, but make sure to bring plenty of good music, because you could be waiting in traffic for a long time. A 2003 study says the city of Miami has the 4th most congested driving conditions in the country.

Famous People from Miami:

Gloria Estefan	Janet Reno
Sidney Poitier	Steve Carlton
Alex Rodriguez	Brett Ratner
Jose Canseco	Vanilla Ice

Local Slang

Laying out – sprawling out under the sun and getting a tan in one of many of the green spaces on campus

The Grove – Short for "Coconut Grove," a collection of clubs and shops about ten minutes away from campus

SoBe – Abbreviation for South Beach, home to many of the area's clubs and restaurants

O.B. – Slang term for the Orange Bowl, UM's historic football stadium and former home of the Miami Dolphins

Students Speak Out On...
Local Atmosphere

{ **"The town is amazing. There are lots of restaurants mostly. I don't attend much, but I hear the club and party scene is extensive."**

Q "**There are a few neighborhoods to avoid**, but it's like any town anywhere in America."

Q "Miami is a very fast-paced city. **There is always something to do.** I would recommend going to Coconut Grove many times, South Beach once, and always avoid Grand Avenue. Coconut Grove is always a fun place to shop, eat, and catch a movie. South Beach is fun to people-watch and spend $100 on your individual meal!"

Q "**Miami is a very aesthetic place.** The look is all that matters."

Q "**The atmosphere of the city is one of the main draws of the university.** It truly is a city that never sleeps. You can always find a place to go and eat or party. If you want to drink, be 21 or have a fake ID that looks good. FIU and FAU also are near our campus, however I do not really see students from there."

Q "There are areas where it is dangerous and you should not stray from main streets in certain areas, however **for the most part the city is definitely a safe place.**"

Q "**The town is perfect for a college campus.** It has its great spots, good spots, and the ones you need to avoid as well. Other universities are present, and are a noticeable factor in the community. The city atmosphere provides a good cultural, as well as career-oriented, atmosphere."

Q "**The atmosphere here in Miami is great.** It's very lively and there are a lot of things to do all the time, for example clubbing on South Beach, dining out, going to the beach, going to football games, and shopping (Sunset Place and the Grove). FIU is the other big school in the greater Miami area."

Q "**It's a nice party city.** Stay away from the ghettos. Visit the beach, Calle Ocho, and downtown Miami."

Q "**The city of Miami always has something going on**, though for those under 21, things can become a bit limiting at some times. There are other schools around, but not within 20 miles or so. There are many movie theaters, bars, clubs, and general places to hang out. However, there are also a lot of areas to be avoided. The 'ghetto' type areas are obviously at the top of this list, and are probably the easiest to identify and avoid."

The College Prowler Take On...
Local Atmosphere

It's hard not to be impressed by the aura of Miami. Whether it's the authentic Cuban culture in Little Havana or the neon frenzy of South Beach, Miami has plenty to do and see. Sports fans will be impressed by the mixture of professional and collegiate athletics, while entertainment-savvy students will love the music and art scenes. There is definitely not a shortage of things to do, and few cities can match Miami's 24-hour atmosphere. There are things to watch out for, including some bad neighborhoods and insane traffic, but the positives far outweigh the negatives when it comes to Miami's atmosphere.

One of the negatives of having such a great city around the campus is that a "college town" has never been born. Colleges in rural areas usually tend to have small cities spring up around them to accommodate the thousands of students. With so much to do around town, Coral Gables seems to be carrying on daily without thinking too much about the big college next door. Miami is a great city for almost anyone, which is why tourism plays such an important part of the culture. Tourists flock to the beautiful beaches, endless shops in Coconut Grove, and to the clubs and bars of South Beach. They may get a little annoying sometimes, but if you end up going to UM, just remember that you used to be one of them.

The College Prowler™ Grade on

Local Atmosphere: A

A high Local Atmosphere grade indicates that the area surrounding campus is safe and scenic. Other factors include nearby attractions, proximity to other schools, and the town's attitude toward students

Safety & Security

The Lowdown On...
Safety & Security

Number of University of Miami Police:
Not Available

UM Police Phone:
(305) 284-6666

Safety Services:
R.A.D
Adopt-A-Cop
Escort
Security Request
Emergency Phones
Silent Witness

Health Services:
Allergy injections
Immunizations
Lab work
X-rays
Primary Care
On-site Pharmaceuticals
Counseling & Psychological Services
STD Screenings
Pregnancy Testing

Health Center Office Hours
Monday, Tuesday, Wednesday, and Friday 8:30 a.m.-5 p.m.,
Thursday 9 a.m.–5 p.m.

Did You Know?
After 10 p.m., no one is allowed into the residential colleges unless they are a resident or are signed in by a resident.

- There are **over seventy emergency phones** located throughout campus. The phones are easy to spot because of their blue lights and dial directly to the Department of Public Safety.

- The **Student Health Center** administers flu shots and common immunizations at various times through the year. They'll even come to you, as part of a program that gives flu shots outside all of the dorms at the beginning of flu season every year.

Students Speak Out On...
Safety & Security

> "Security is maintained at a fairly high level. Check-in booths at all entrances ensure safety after 10 p.m. Moreover, you must swipe your ID at three locations before you may enter your dorm after 10 p.m., so there is a real sense of safety, especially in the nighttime hours."

Q "**I have felt safe all five years here on campus**, but then again, I am a male. I have heard stories about ladies not feeling safe and I walk them home late at night."

Q "**The campus is very secure.** There are several places on campus that have emergency phones in case an emergency ever arises. Also, police are always walking or driving around campus. After 10 p.m. each student entering a residential college must present their ID to make sure they live in that college. People that do not have proper identification must be signed in prior to entering a residential college. I have always felt very safe at the university."

Q "I feel very safe and secure on this campus, regardless of the incident reports we get about crimes. They're very rare and I haven't heard of a problem in months. It is a big city, so **there is some need for concern, but I feel very safe here**."

Q "**Safety is fairly good** considering that the area the campus is located in is fairly safe anyway."

Q "**I feel perfectly safe walking around on campus any time of the day or night alone.** Still, we sometimes get reports in E-mails about some crime going on on campus that we should watch out for."

Q "I would say that **the security on the UM campus is above average** and that our campus is in a safe neighborhood. I'm not worried by E-mails regarding crimes that happened on campus. Actually I'm proud to have our school post warnings like that to let us be aware of what's going on."

Q "**Security seems adequate.** I have never felt unsafe walking back to the dorms alone at 2 a.m., but that may just be the kind of person I am."

Q "I believe that **security on campus does vary based on gender**. If you are a guy, it does not really matter, however some girls feel that walking alone at night is not the most safe thing to do. I believe that the campus is pretty safe and have not felt insecure yet."

The College Prowler Take On...
Safety & Security

The majority of students on campus feel safe walking around at night, and there are tons of cops and security guards, as well as emergency phones in case there is ever a problem. Even though Miami can certainly be a dangerous city at times, UM is located in Coral Gables, which is a fairly nice neighborhood. Still, this doesn't hide the fact that several incidences have occurred on campus in recent years. The crimes that were committed, which included burglary and sexual assault, were recognized because of UM's policy of E-mailing the entire student body whenever a serious crime occurs on campus. This is a practice that is not in effect at most of the country's universities. It makes students aware of problems that may exist, though the amount of students outside late at night rarely changes after one of these alerts.

Although UM officials are very concerned with crime on campus and heavily investigate any threats, it's important for students to know that crime is, at times, an issue. The Department of Public Safety should be commended for its honesty about what's happening around campus. The department's truthfulness in these matters makes students feel more comfortable walking around at night. No matter how many police officers the school hires, however, there will always be a risk. The most important thing is that an overwhelming majority of students feel safe on campus, and that there is very little risk of extremely serious crimes.

The College Prowler™ Grade on

Safety & Security: B

A high grade in Safety & Security means that students generally feel safe, campus police are visible, blue-light phones and escort services are readily available, and safety precautions are not overly necessary.

Computers

The Lowdown On...
Computers

High-Speed Network?
Yes

Wireless Network?
Yes

Number of Labs:
7 IT-supported labs, over 60 total labs

Number of Computers:
218 in IT-supported labs

Operating Systems:
PC

Free Software:
Symantec AntiVirus, Windows XP Professional Upgrade, Microsoft Office, Microsoft Frontpage, Publisher 2002, Visual Studio

Discounted Software
None

24-Hour Labs
None (except during exams)

Charge to Print?
No

Did You Know?
The school library alone contains **128 computers** with Internet access and free printing to one of ten printers.

• Every residential college on campus has a computer lab in its lobby, complete with **free printing** and a staff member on site to assist with problems.

Students Speak Out On...
Computers

"I would recommend having your own computer so that you do not have to depend on another source. Computer labs are generally full. The computer network is very good, but sometimes, unfortunately, the network is down. When that happens, within a few hours it is back up."

Q "The computer network is great, but typical to any college setting. **High speed internet and access to the school's databases are readily accessible**. I do not frequent the computer labs, however I would advise bringing your own computer because it makes life easier to know that you don't have to go hunting for a place to type up an essay or whatever."

Q "The computer network is quite good, and there is wireless throughout the campus. The library is sometimes full. **Definitely bring your own computer**."

Q "The Internet works on a cable connection and is pretty fast on most occasions. There are many computers around campus that are accessible and open, but **I would say to still bring your own compute**r. It is just that much easier to work whenever you need to get something done."

Q "**Computer labs are crowded late at night**, but during the day it's not hard to get access to one. However, I would still recommend that everyone have his own computer because of convenience. If you need to write a paper the night before it's due, you really can't trust that there's going to be a computer available."

Q "**Most people bring their own computers** because it's nice to have one in your room, but a lot of people print stuff out at the labs because, unlike some other schools, it's free here. Sometimes the computers kick you off of AIM or the whole internet for a while, but it's probably not that often."

Q "It's always nice to have your own computer for those last minute papers. However, you can easily get by without one, because all the residential halls have them. **The computers are way too crowded at the library**."

Q "The network is okay, but **you can't use Kazaa and such anymore**."

Q "The computers are good, except **in the library you sometimes have to wait foreve**r to get a turn using them during the day."

Q "If you are an architecture student like I am, **the lab is usually busy during exam week.** Otherwise, there are plenty of computers."

Q "**The computer network has its ups and downs.** Most of the problems are caused by the school's never-ending quest to halt file-sharing programs. The computer labs are open enough time during the week to get important work done, and there are enough of them so that they are not constantly crowded. If the dorm labs are full, however, the library also has a large bank of computers. But, what kind of modern college student doesn't come with a computer these days, anyway?"

Q "**Our computer labs are generally never full**. They are very nice and conducive to studying."

The College Prowler Take On...
Computers

Movies like *Terminator* and *The Matrix* predict that computers will someday take over earth and enslave the human race. What better reason could there be for keeping one in your dorm room? Having a computer in college is more of a social luxury than an academic necessity. Computer labs can be found in the lobby of every UM residence hall, as well as the library, and they're hardly ever full. It's much more convenient, however, to lay in bed like a lazy walrus with a laptop and finish your homework that way. Those who can afford it should bring a computer to college. A laptop with a long cord is a plus, because then, if you have a fridge close by and a strong bladder, there will be no reason to ever get out of bed on the weekends.

Like most colleges, UM has a fast and fairly reliable network that gives you easy access to the Internet, and the campus-wide wireless network is a huge asset if you have a laptop. The system does go down occasionally, but almost always comes back within a few minutes. For students looking to cut back on spending, rest assured that you can complete your assignments in the computer labs. They stay open late, some past midnight, and always have a dillusional staff member there to help with technical problems. But the majority of students who use the labs are only there to save their own printers' ink or to fulfill the requirements of archaic professors who still want assignments saved on floppy disks, a feature left off many modern computers.

The College Prowler™ Grade on

Computers: B

A high grade in Computers designates that computer labs are available, the computer network is easily accessible, and the campus' computing technology is up-to-date.

Facilities

The Lowdown On...
Facilities

Student Center:
The Whitten University Center (UC)

Athletic Center:
Wellness Center, Hecht Athletic Center, IM Fields

Libraries:
12

Popular Places to Chill:
The UC
The Rat
The Rock
UC Patio
Storm Surge Cafe

Campus Size in Acres:
260 acres

What Is There to Do On Campus?

The Wellness Center is a newly renovated, state-of-the-art gym located near two of the residential colleges. Access is free to students, making it a great place for health-conscious students and those just looking to play some basketball or take a swim. There are also free movies for students at the campus theater, comedians and musicians at the Rathskellar, and top touring bands at the newly built Convocation Center, which doubles as a basketball arena.

Movie Theatre on Campus?

Yes. Bill Cosford Cinema, Memorial Building

Bowling on Campus?

No

Bar on Campus?

Yes. The Rathskellar (also hosts live bands and comedians)

Coffeehouse on Campus?

Yes. The Coffee Company (Starbucks), Hurricane Food Court (closes early though)

Favorite Things to Do:

Some students gather in the Storm Surge Café at the UC to shoot pool or play ping-pong. Others enjoy working out at the Wellness Center or playing sports on the massive IM Fields. Of course, there are also numerous Division 1A sporting events on and off campus, all of which are free to UM students with their ID cards.

Students Speak Out On...
Facilities

"The facilities, which span all interests, are all top-notch. The Wellness Center is top-of-the-line, sporting amenities for any activity one may seek to pursue. The bookstore, university center, and dining halls are all clean and technologically sound."

Q "The buildings are uglier than sin, but the landscape makes up for them. **Inside, most of the major buildings are very nicely decorated** and kept-up and you forget what the outside looks like. The new buildings are nicely designed."

Q "**The facilities are very nice.** The Wellness Center offers students the opportunity to lift weights, play basketball, volleyball, and racquetball, run, and swim. The library has a wide variety of sources for students to access. The Whitten University Center is a nice place for students to just sit around and relax. The Storm Surge Café is a place where students can hang out, play billiards, and eat. The UC also has a lap pool for students to work on their tan."

Q "The facilities vary. **The Wellness Center is beautiful and is a great place to work out**, with three floors, including indoor and outdoor basketball courts, an indoor pool, hot tub and sauna, and all the workout equipment you can think of. The classroom buildings vary as well. Some are old but still get the job done. Others are brand new and beautiful. The student center is OK, but I don't really go there often."

Q "**The facilities on campus are ridiculously nice.** They're all either brand new or newly renovated. For instance, our Wellness Center is under five years old and unbelievable. The women you can meet their are equally unbelievable. I'm losing my mind!"

Q "The facilities are alright. **The athletic and computer areas are very nice**."

Q "**The Wellness Center is amazing** and has a zillion aerobics classes. I've tried some at other schools and they're much better here and offered at more times."

Q "**The student center isn't as nice as at other schools,** but they are supposedly renovating that pretty soon."

Q "There are really nice facilities here. **The Wellness Center is awesome.**"

Q "**The fitness facilities are outstanding, some of the best I have ever seen.** While I usually prefer to do my workouts outside, the gym is equipped with everything someone would need (indoor track, indoor pool, sauna, classrooms for any class-type workouts like yoga, racquetball courts, volleyball courts, the fully equipped weight and cardio section, and a juice bar). The student center is adequate, with many places to eat or talk to friends."

The College Prowler Take On...
Facilities

Although most of the classroom buildings around UM are hideously ugly, the insides are generally decent and the new buildings are very nice. The highlight of UM's facilities is, by far, the Wellness Center – a huge gym located next to the dorms where most freshmen live. The building stays open until midnight on weeknights, allowing for late night games of basketball, squash, or racquetball, which can provide a great study break. The multi-level gym has pretty much anything a student could want, and this is definitely something to look forward to when coming to UM. The other place where students spend a lot of time is the University Center, aptly located in the center of campus. The UC has a lounge with television, an information desk, food court, offices, and a convenience store, and is attached to the bookstore and campus post office.

The UC is a nice enough place, although it lacks some cool features that are present at other schools, like a bowling alley. There is a movie theater in a corner of campus that shows relatively new movies free to students, as well as art-house fare. Students seem to appreciate the campus facilities, especially the Wellness Center, but any new renovations to the UC or campus buildings would certainly be welcome. The good news is that UM is always making changes and improvements, and if something is getting run down or old, it's likely to be updated soon.

The College Prowler™ Grade on

Facilities: B+

A high Facilities grade indicates that the campus is aesthetically pleasing and well-maintained; facilities are state-of-the-art, and libraries are exceptional. Other determining factors include the quality of both athletic and student centers and an abundance of things to do on campus.

Campus Dining

The Lowdown On...
Campus Dining

Freshman Meal Plan Requirement?
Yes

Meal Plan Average Cost:
$3,318 a year

Places to Grab a Bite with Your Meal Plan

Burger King
Hurricane Food Court
Food:
American fast food
Favorite Dish:
Whopper with Cheese
Hours:
Monday-Thursday 7 a.m.-8 p.m., Friday 7 a.m.-4 p.m.

The Coffee Company (Starbucks)

Hurricane Food Court

Food:
Coffee/Pastries

Favorite Dish:
Various Coffee

Hours:
Monday-Thursday 7 a.m.-5 p.m., Friday 7 a.m.-4 p.m.

Convenience Store

UC

Food:
Snack Food

Favorite Dish:
Krispy Kreme Donuts

Hours:
Monday-Thursday 7 a.m.-2 a.m., Friday 7 a.m.-4 a.m., Saturday 9 a.m.-4 a.m.

Crepemaker

Outside the UC

Food:
Crepes

Favorite Dish:
Caesar Chicken Crepe

Hours:
Monday-Friday 8:30 a.m.-3 p.m.

Jamba Juice

Hurricane Food Court

Food:
Smoothies

Favorite Dish:
Orange-A-Peel

Hours:
Monday-Thursday 9 a.m.-8 p.m., Friday 9 a.m.-4 p.m.

Juice Bar

Wellness Center

Food:
Drinks/Smoothies

Favorite Dish:
Orange Creamsicle

Hours:
Monday-Friday 7:30 a.m.-10 p.m., Saturday-Sunday 11 a.m.-5 p.m.

Leo's Deli

Hurricane Food Court

Food:
Sandwiches/Soups

Favorite Dish:
Texas Cheddar Melt

Hours:
Monday-Thursday 10:30 a.m.-6 p.m., Friday 10:30 a.m.-4 p.m.

Mahoney/Pearson Dining Hall

Next to Mahoney/Pearson Residential College

Food:
Buffet

Favorite Dish:
Omelettes

Hours:
Monday-Thursday 7 a.m.-9 p.m., Friday 7 a.m.-7 p.m., Saturday 9 a.m.-7 p.m., Sunday 11 a.m.-7 p.m.

Market Square

Hurricane Food Court

Food:
Salad Bar/Soups

Favorite Dish:
Soup of the Day

Market Square (*Continued...*)
Hours:
Monday-Friday 11 a.m.-4 p.m.

Panda Express
Hurricane Food Court
Food:
Chinese
Favorite Dish:
Mandarin Chicken
Hours:
Monday-Thursday 11 a.m.-6
p.m., Friday 11 a.m.-4 p.m.

Rathskellar
Next to Hurricane Food Court
Food:
Bar food
Favorite Dish:
Chicken Tenders with Fries
Hours:
Monday-Friday 11 a.m.-10
p.m., Sunday 12 p.m.-8 p.m.
(during football season only)

Sbarro's
UC
Food:
Pizza/Italian
Favorite Dish:
Cheese Pizza
Hours:
Monday-Sunday
11 a.m.-12 a.m.

Subway
Law School
Food:
Sandwiches
Favorite Dish:
Meatball Sub

Subway (*Continued...*)
Hours:
Monday-Thursday 7 a.m.-10
p.m., Friday 7 a.m.-7 p.m.,
Saturday 10 a.m.-7 p.m.,
Sunday 11 a.m.-7 p.m.

Storm Surge Cafe
Snack Food
Food:
Bar food/American
Favorite Dish:
Turkey Sandwich
Hours:
Monday-Thursday 9 a.m.-11
p.m., Friday 9 a.m.-9 p.m.,
Saturday 11 a.m.-5 p.m.,
Sunday 11 a.m.-11 p.m.

Snack Carts
Various walkways and
courtyards around campus
Food:
Chips, cookies, soda, and
other snacks for between
classes
Favorite Dish:
Pop Tarts
Hours:
Monday-Friday 8 a.m.-2 p.m.

Stanford Dining Hall
Next to Stanford Residential
College
Food:
Buffet
Favorite Dish:
Omelettes
Hours:
Monday-Thursday 7 a.m.-9
p.m., Friday 7 a.m.-7 p.m.,
Saturday 9 a.m.-7 p.m.

Tsunami Sushi
Hurricane Food Court

Food:
Sushi

Favorite Dish:
Marina Plate

Hours:
Monday-Friday 11 a.m.-4 p.m.

World's Fare
Hurricane Food Court

Food:
Various ethnic foods

Favorite Dish:
Rotisserie Chicken with Macaroni and Cheese

Hours:
Monday-Friday 11 a.m.-4 p.m.

Did You Know?
The dining halls stay open late once per semester for a "**midnight breakfast**" to help students who are up late studying for final exams.

• The dining halls are stocked with current issues of the student newspaper, as well as free copies of the local papers and *USA Today* for students to **read while eating**.

Student Favorites
Subway, Sbarro's, The Rathskellar, Jamba Juice

Other Options
Most of the places in the food court are only open for lunch, but Sbarro's, Subway, Burger King, and The Rat are usually open later.

Students Speak Out On...
Campus Dining

{ **"Dining halls are dining halls, anywhere you go. The food court is great and the Rat is a great place to chill in between classes and shoot some pool."**

Q "**The dining hall food is annoying and repetitive,** plain and simple. After about the first month as a freshman you're ready to kill yourself. However, the university does have a "center" that has many fast food-type establishments, offering a change from the everyday monotony of dining hall food."

Q "My favorite place to eat on campus is at Panda Express. I am a fan of Chinese/Japanese food. **The dining hall food is good, but it is very repetitive.** You are always guaranteed that chicken, mashed potatoes, stir fry, and a burger will be on the menu. I have not been too disappointed with the on-campus dining."

Q "The food on campus varies depending on where you eat. The dining dollars used at places like Taco Bell, Panda Express, Subway, and fast food places are always a good choice for the lazy college student, but **the real dining hall gets really old quick**. It serves the same dishes many times in the week and it feels like the food they get is not always the best quality. I have friends who have boycotted the cafeteria for long periods of time."

Q "**Residential dining is respectable, but gets old very quickly.** If your parents were good cooks, you probably won't like it, but if they weren't, you'll be impressed."

Q "**The food does get old after a while.** Fast food restaurants on campus are hot spots, with names like Taco Bell, Sbarro's, and Subway."

Q "Food in the food courts is alright, although sometimes not as good as at the same places off campus. **The dining hall is horrible**."

Q "I like the dining halls because **there are a lot of choices** and you can either eat healthfully or not, whatever you like. Besides the dining halls, dining on campus gets really boring because there is only one other food court and the menu there doesn't vary much. We do have an on-campus Friday's-type place, the Rat."

Q "The dining hall food is alright. **It gets repetitive**, but the Stanford Dining Hall is really nice. The food court is nice. At the food court there is a Taco Bell, Burger King, a sandwich place, Chinese food, sushi bar, juice place, mini-Starbucks, and an ethnic food place."

Q "**The dining halls are, contrary to popular belief, actually not that bad**. The food quality itself is usually decent (though the menu gets repetitive). If the dining halls are not what someone wants, there is also the on-campus Subway, Burger King, Taco Bell, Starbucks, Jamba Juice, Sbarro's, Panda Express, and more."

The College Prowler Take On...
Campus Dining

The school has two dining halls, both with pretty standard college buffet food. The variety sounds good – pizza, pastas, made-to-order sandwiches, hamburgers, hot dogs, fries, salad, and ice cream are only a few of the daily staples – but nothing is of very high quality. Most students don't mind the food at first, but get really sick of it sometime around Halloween in their freshman year. This is about how long it takes to realize that all the different foods have the same greasy taste. Even the salad and the ice cream are almost indistinguishable if you don't look at them.

Freshmen usually start with the comfortable 14 meal plan, which cost $3,318 for the 2004/2005 school year and allows for 14 meals at the dining hall per week. Unless you were raised on Sizzler, then you'll probably drop that to the 8 meal plan for your second semester, which is the minimum UM allows for a student living on campus. Either plan gives the student "dining dollars" that can be used like a credit card at the restaurants on campus. The 14 meal plan comes with $150 dining dollars per semester, and the 8 meal plan gets you $200. This money is pretty valuable, because UM has an excellent selection of fast food restaurants on campus. There's a food court with Taco Bell, Panda Express, Burger King, Jamba Juice, and Starbucks, and there's even an overpriced takeout sushi bar if you feel like blowing all your dining dollars on the first day. Other places to eat include a Sbarro, a Subway, a crepe stand, and the Rathskeller – a sports bar and popular meeting place. If you don't use all of your dining dollars by the end of the semester, you can always head over to the campus convenience store and spend the remainder on junk food and prehistoric donuts.

The College Prowler™ Grade on
Campus Dining: C+

Our grade on Campus Dining addresses the quality of both school-owned dining halls and independent on-campus restaurants as well as the price, availability, and variety of food.

Off-Campus Dining

The Lowdown On...
Off-Campus Dining

Restaurant Prowler:
Popular Places to Eat!

La Carreta
3632 SW 8th St.
Calle Ocho
(305) 444-7501
Food: Cuban
Cool Features: Massive slices of pizza available for delivery.
Price: $10 and under per person
Hours: 24 hours

Casola's
2437 SW 17th Ave., Miami
(305) 858-0090
Food: Italian
Cool Features: Massive slices of pizza available for delivery.
Price: $10 and under per person
Hours: Monday-Thursday 11 a.m.-2 a.m., Friday-Saturday 11 a.m.-4 a.m., Sunday 11 a.m.-1 a.m.

Cheesecake Factory
7497 Dadeland Mall,
South Miami/Kendall
(305) 665-6400
Food: American
Cool Features: Order dessert
from a long list of flavored
cheesecakes
Price: $20 and under per
person
Hours: Monday-Thursday 11:30
a.m.-11 p.m., Friday-Saturday
11:30 a.m.-12:30 a.m., Sunday
10 a.m.-11 p.m

Chicken Kitchen
7315 Red Road
South Miami
(305) 669-0099
Food: Spanish, Cuban Fast
Food
Cool Features: Serves
traditional Chicken-style dishes

Price: Monday-Sunday 11 a.m.-
11 p.m.

Denny's
1150 South Dixie Hwy.

(305) 666-6250

Food: American

Cool Features: The only 24-
hour dining within walking
distance of campus.

Price: $8 and under per person

Hours: 24 hours

Friday's
1200 South Dixie Hwy.,
(305) 668-7808

Fax: (305) 668-3853

Food: American/Family

Cool Features: Watch live
sports games in the bar area

Friday's (Continued...)
Price: $12 and under
Hours: Monday-Thursday 11
a.m.-1 a.m., Friday-Saturday 11
a.m.-2 a.m., Sunday 11 a.m.-12
a.m.

Havana Harry's
4612 South LeJeune Rd
(305) 661-2622
Food: Cuban/Spanish
Price: $20 and under per
person
Hours: Monday-Friday
11 a.m.-10 p.m., Saturday 12
p.m.-11 p.m., Sunday 5 p.m.-
11 p.m.

Jerry's Famous Deli
1450 Collins Ave., South Beach
(305) 532-8030
Food: Sandwiches/Deli
Price: $15 and under per
person
Hours: 24 hours

Johnny Rocket's
5701 Sunset Dr.
Sunset Place
(305) 663-1004
Food: American
Cool Features: Throwback to
the 50's craze of burgers, fries,
and shakes.
Price: $10 and under per
person
Hours: Monday-Thursday 11
a.m.-10 p.m., Friday-Saturday
11 a.m.-12 a.m., Sunday 11
a.m.-10 p.m.

Miami's Best Pizza
1514 South Dixie Hwy
(305) 666-5931

Miami's Best Pizza (Cont'...)

Food: Italian
Cool Features: Offers delivery
Price: $8 and under per person
Hours: Sunday-Wednesday
11 a.m.–1 a.m., Thursday 11
a.m.-2 a.m., Friday-Saturday 11
a.m.-3 a.m.

Riviera Pizza

1558 South Dixie Hwy
(305) 666-3730
Food: Italian
Cool Features: Special pizza
deal for UM students. Also
delivers.
Price: $6 and under per person
Hours: Monday-Sunday 11
a.m.-12 a.m.

Swenson's

1586 South Dixie Hwy
(305) 661-7658
Food: American/Ice Cream
Cool Features: Famous for old-
fashioned ice cream sundaes.
Price: $9 and under per person
Hours: Monday-Thursday 11
a.m.-11 p.m., Friday-Saturday
11 a.m.-1 a.m., Sunday 12
p.m.-11 p.m.

Texas Taco Factory

475 South Dixie Hwy., Coral
Gables

(305) 662-2212

Food: Mexican

Cool Features: Delivery, drive-
thru, and dining room.

Price: $10 and under per
person

Hours: Monday-Thursday 12
p.m.-2 a.m., Friday-Saturday
12 p.m.-4 a.m.

Sunset Tavern

7232 SW 59th Ave., South
Miami

(305) 665-9996

Food: American

Price: $10 and under per
person

Hours: Monday-Sunday 11
a.m.-3 a.m.

Versailles

3555 SW 8th St.
Calle Ocho
(305) 445-7614
Fax: (305) 444-7546
Food: Cuban
Cool Features: Massive slices
of pizza available for delivery.
Price: $10 and under per
person
Hours: Monday-Sunday 7 a.m.-
2 a.m.

Best Pizza:

Miami's Best Pizza
Riviera Pizza
Casola's

Best Breakfast:

Denny's
Jerry's Famous Deli

Best Wings:

Hooters
Kendall Ale House

Best Healthy:

Wild Oats Marktplace

Best Place to Take Your Parents:

Havana Harry's
Cheesecake Factory

Student Favorites

Denny's, Friday's, Texas Taco
Factory, Casola's, Miami's Best
Pizza'

Closest Grocery Stores:

Publix
1401 Monza Ave.
Coral Gables, across from
campus
(305) 667-1681

Winn-Dixie
5850 SW 73rd St.
South Miami
behind Sunset Place
(305) 666-5241

Did You Know?

24-Hour Eating
Denny's, Jerry's Famous Deli, La Carreta,
McDonalds, Taco Bell

Fun Facts
• Some of the best bars around Miami also **double as trendy restaurants** during the day and early evening.

• For a massive selection of late-night dining, take a 20-minute drive over the bridge to South Beach, where **nothing closes early**.

• Every spring, celebrity chefs flock to Miami for the **South Beach Wine & Food Festival**. Past guests have included Food Network favorites Emeril Lagasse and Bobby Flay.

Students Speak Out On...
Off-Campus Dining

"There are tons of places to dine off-campus. No matter what kind of food you are looking for, there will be at least one place serving it. Among many, my top choices are Japanese (i.e. sushi: Somoto, Taisho, etc.), Thai (The Lotus Room), and good old American (Ale House, etc.)."

"Well, **Miami is known for its ethnic food,** such as Cuban like Havana Harry's and Versailles. Other great restaurants are on South Beach and downtown Coral Gables. The best authentic steakhouse is Porcao in downtown Miami."

"**Miami has a variety of restaurants that are worth trying**; my favorite is Lario's, located behind Sunset Place. If you go, go on Friday and Saturday night after 11 p.m. to hear the live salsa band perform. The singer sounds exactly like the famous Cuban singer Celia Cruz. Also, Versailles is another excellent Cuban restaurant. If you are in the mood for seafood, Monty's is a great bar and seafood restaurant, but it is a little bit pricey. Other favorites include Friday's and The Ale House."

"One word...MIAMI. **Some of the best food in the world is found in this city.** From delis to Cuban food, you can't miss. The only problem is it does get a little pricey at times. Some of the best are places like Rascal House (a deli), Havana Harry's (Cuban), and Versailles (Cuban). Then of course there are the regulars like Friday's, Denny's and others."

Q "**The restaurants off campus are great.** There are so many good places: Pizza Rustica on South Beach, Havana Harry's, etc."

Q "The Friday's across the street is by far one of the worst I have ever been to. The service is ridiculously slow. **I prefer to go to the Cheesecake Factory.** There are two locations pretty nearby and one that you can get to on the Thursday-Saturday night shuttle."

Q "Since I don't have a car, **Friday's and Denny's are the two fine dining establishments near campus**."

Q "**This is Miami, there are excellent restaurants everywhere.** Some highly recommended places within walking distance to the school would include Titanic Brewery, Dan Marino's, Johnny Rocket's, The Big Cheese, and various other chains of restaurants. If someone has more expensive tastes, there is always South Beach (which has a MUCH larger variety , ranging from the always excellent Jerry's Deli to NexxtCafe)."

The College Prowler Take On...
Off-Campus Dining

There aren't many cities that can match Miami as far as restaurants go. There is basically an endless amount of new places to try, and thankfully the quality of the restaurants matches up with the quantity of them. If you usually eat around Sunset Place or on US-1, you can always head to Coconut Grove, South Beach, or downtown Coral Gables for a totally different selection of restaurants. All of these areas have numerous great restaurants, ranging from casual, cheap pizza and bar food to expensive seafood or Italian. Students with cars like eating in the Grove, which also has shops, a movie theater, and lots of bars, providing for plenty of after-dinner entertainment. Even students without transportation will be impressed by the off campus dining. There are dozens of restaurants right across the street at Sunset Place and in the surrounding area, not to mention what else becomes available if you're willing to risk a Metrorail ride.

Most students come to school without knowing a lot about Miami restaurants, and then they fall in love with a couple and frequent them for the next four years. The great thing about off campus dining is that there is delivery available from so many places that almost every type of food can be covered. There are of course many quality pizza places that deliver to UM until late at night. There are also Mexican, Chinese, and Cuban restaurants that deliver. For quick 24 hour dining, it's about a five minute to drive to Taco Bell or McDonalds. For larger meals at all hours, look for Denny's across the street, La Carreta and its various neighbors on Calle Ocho, or Jerry's Deli in South Beach, where there's never a shortage of things to do at any hour of the day.

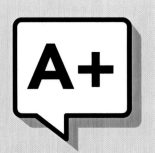

The College Prowler™ Grade on

Off-Campus Dining: A+

A high off-campus dining grade implies that off-campus restaurants are affordable, accessible, and worth visiting. Other factors include the variety of cuisine and the availability of alternative options (vegetarian, vegan, Kosher, etc.).

On-Campus Housing

The Lowdown On...
On-Campus Housing

Room Types:
Residential colleges have either standard rooms or suites.

Standard—Each floor contains a large, multiple-person bathroom that is shared by about 40 students (most freshman are placed in these halls)

Suite—Two rooms with two students in each share a connecting bathroom

On-campus apartments can have two or three bedrooms and hold up to six students who share kitchen and bathroom facilities.

Best Dorms:
Mahoney

Pearson

Eaton

Worst Dorms:
Hecht

Stanford

(Both also known as "the Towers")

Dormitory Residences

Apartment Area

Floors: 3

Number of Occupants: Not Available

Bathrooms: In-Room

Co-Ed: Yes

Room Types: Apartments

Special Features: No Freshmen students, Laundry Facilities Between Apartments

Eaton College

Floors: 4

Number of Occupants: approximately 400

Bathrooms: Shared Between Rooms

Co-Ed: Yes

Room Types: Suite Single, Suite Double

Special Features: Laundry, Study Lounges on every floor

Hecht College

Floors: Two towers with 12 floors each
Number of Occupants: Approximately 700

Bathrooms: Shared By Floor

Co-Ed: Yes

Room Types: Standard Single, Standard Double

Special Features: Laundry, Study Lounge in Lobby

Mahoney College

Floors: 7

Number of Occupants: Approximately 700

Bathrooms: Shared Between Rooms

Co-Ed: Yes

Room Types: Suite Single, Suite Double

Special Features:Laundry, Study Lounges, Kitchens Shared by Floor

Pearson College

Floors: 7

Number of Occupants: approximately 700

Bathrooms: Shared Between Rooms

Co-Ed: Yes

Room Types: Suite Single, Suite Double

Special Features: Laundry, Study Lounges, Kitchens Shared By Floor

Stanford College

Floors: Two towers with 12 floors each

Number of Occupants: approximately 700

Bathrooms: Shared By Floor

Co-Ed: Yes

Room Types: Standard Single, Standard Double

Special Features: Laundry, Study Lounge in Lobby

Number of University Owned Apartments:

35

Undergrads on Campus:

41%

Number of Dormitories:

5 (not including apartments)

Bed Type

Twin extra long (39"x80")

Available for Rent

N/A

Cleaning Service?

In public areas. Floor bathrooms, study lounges, hallways, and common areas are cleaned daily by staff. Shared bathrooms between suites are not cleaned by staff

What You Get

Bed, desk and chair, dresser, bookshelf, closet space, trash can, window coverings, cable TV connection, Ethernet connection, free campus and local phone calls (phone not included)

Also Available

Quiet floors, cart and vacuum loans

Did You Know?

• The campus cable network was upgraded recently to include **HBO and 60 other stations** that are free to students.

• There is at least **one Resident Assistant living on each floor** whose job it is to help new students feel comfortable and encourage friendly relations among floormates.

• Under a newly passed law in Florida, there is **no smoking allowed in campus buildings**, including the residential colleges. Picnic tables and benches are set up for smokers outside of each dorm.

Students Speak Out On...
On-Campus Housing

"The dorms are typical, yet quite nice. I think it is impossible to avoid the community bathroom 'freshmen dorms,' but once the first year is over, Eaton, Mahoney, and Pearson sport double suite-type rooms (each with their own bathroom), which are typically more sought-after by students here."

Q "I like the dorm life. **It's the easiest time in the world to meet random people.** I lived in Hecht for freshman year and loved it because there are a large variety of people. I heard Mahoney is where all the pretty people live with all the athletes and Eaton is the place to live if you want somewhere in between."

Q "I do not mind the dorms at all. In fact, I **strongly recommend living on campus.** It has been a lot of fun living with several people of different backgrounds, and I have enjoyed getting to know all of them. Some people complain about communal bathrooms, but they are cleaned twice a day. Other people complain about roommates, but I have not had a bad experience with my roommate."

Q "**Dorms are nice but small, as they are everywhere**. I highly recommend freshman live in Stanford and Hecht, aptly named the Towers, to meet people. Nicer dorms exist across campus at Mahoney, Pearson, and Eaton, which are suites. The Towers have community bathrooms."

Q "**The dorms are alright.** Eaton's a nice place to live after freshman year if you like it quiet. Mahoney/Pearson is more social than Eaton."

Q "Most freshmen live in the Towers and they're not as bad as you would imagine. They have bathrooms down the hall, but **they're generally really clean for shared bathrooms**. Then, there are the suite-style rooms which involve cleaning your own bathroom. That kind of sucks, but the rooms are much better shaped and brighter. There are also on-campus apartments."

Q "The dorms are livable. The towers (Stanford and Hecht) are generally less sought-after due to the communal bathrooms, **but have a much better social atmosphere.** The suites (Eaton, Pearson, and Mahoney) have one bathroom per two rooms, and are a bit larger, but offer a much less social atmosphere."

Q "I'm an R.A. and **I find the dorms to be pretty nice** and, more importantly, convenient."

Q "**The dorms are a great environment**. There are freshman dorms (Stanford and Hecht), which were a really fun time. They are co-ed by floor, and the rooms are doubles. There really is not a set of dorms to stay away from; they are pretty much all the same set up. I currently reside in Eaton Residential College, which is for sophomores and upper classmen. It is a suite setup and connects through the restroom."

Q "I like living on campus and **all of the benefits that come with it**, which include waking up and going to class without worrying about parking, and meeting more people through the residence halls."

The College Prowler Take On...
On-Campus Housing

If you decide to attend UM, there will be a form you fill out ranking the residential colleges by preference. This seems to be basically useless, as almost all freshmen are placed in Hecht or Stanford, also called the Towers. Almost everyone lives in the Towers for their first year. Although the other dorms are bigger and don't have whole-floor bathrooms, most students agree that spending a year in the Towers is a good experience because it forces you to meet people. Although almost everyone agrees that the suites in Mahoney, Pearson, and Eaton are nicer, some students like the atmosphere in the Towers so much that they keep their rooms for the next year. The Towers are definitely the most wild and fun dorms, then come Mahoney and Pearson, where some floors have a good social atmosphere. Eaton is generally considered the quietest of the residential colleges, which some people love.

If you're lucky and you have a good RA, your floor will turn into a big family. Video game tournaments and hallway sports are common, and chances are at least a few people on your floor will be friends that you keep in touch with for the rest of college. A lot of upperclassmen try to get into the apartments, which are tough to reserve. The layout is nice, but the buildings themselves are old and are in random areas of campus where it's hard to meet new people. In the past, there have been overcrowding issues and students have been sent to the Holiday Inn across the street from campus. Even though a free hotel room with maid service and HBO might sound like a good deal, avoid this at all costs if you have any desire to meet people and make friends.

B-

The College Prowler™ Grade on
Campus Housing: B-

A high Campus Housing grade indicates that dorms are clean, well-maintained, and spacious. Other determining factors include variety of dorms, proximity to classes, and social atmosphere.

Off-Campus Housing

The Lowdown On...
Off-Campus Housing

Undergrads in Off-Campus Housing:
59%

Average Rent for a Studio Apartment:
$650/month

Average Rent for a One-Bedroom Apartment:
$800/month

Average Rent for a Two-Bedroom Apartment:
$1200/month

Popular Areas:
Coral Gables

South Miami

Brickell/Downtown

Best Time to Look for a Place:
Beginning or Middle of 2nd Semester

Students Speak Out On...
Off-Campus Housing

"I lived on campus for four years and in the apartments for three of them. This year I live off campus in downtown Miami, and the commute is fine as long as you live opposing traffic."

Q "I have not considered living off campus, though I have many friends who do live off campus and find it as **a nice change**."

Q "**Off campus housing is easily obtained after freshman year**. It's Miami, a big city that has plenty of places to live and more people willing to rent around the campus. It really depends on whether or not you want to live on or off campus. There are definite benefits to living off campus, including nicer living conditions, but it comes with drawbacks as well."

Q "**Housing off campus is as convenient as being off campus can be.** Parking is annoying, as lots are almost always full and spots hard to find. Like anything, it has its positives and negatives, but at least from my position, more positives, like larger living spaces, better laundry facilities, and lack of students across the hall screaming at 4:00 in the morning."

Q "Housing off campus varies. The most common option is to rent a house with a bunch of friends, and **in most cases it's cheaper than living on campus**."

"**I wouldn't bother with off-campus housing**. Sitting in traffic on US-1 is ridiculous and it takes forever to get to and from campus."

"**If you live off-campus, you have the luxury of your own space,** but it doesn't even remotely come close to the experience of living on campus. You get the chance of meeting people from all walks of life, and besides, that's where all the action is."

"**Off-campus housing is widely available**, because Miami is a big city. It ranges from nice apartments to houses of all sorts."

The College Prowler Take On...
Off-Campus Housing

Off-campus housing is a popular choice among UM's upperclassmen. It seems like a great situation: renting a house off campus can be cheaper than living in the dorms on campus, and they don't force you into a meal plan. Living space in a house is obviously larger than in a dorm room, and having your own place allows for more freedom than living on campus. There are a couple of major negatives though, which is why residential colleges and apartments on campus continue to be popular with upperclassmen. Living off-campus requires a car and a great deal of patience, as Miami traffic is generally awful. Expect to wake up pretty early to make it to school on time, and you'll probably be in for a long walk to class from one of the two garages where most commuters park. Living off-campus also presents a social conflict. On one hand, you'd be able to have parties and more people over with the larger living space. But you won't have neighbors to hang out with like you do in the dorms, and you can't just walk outside and down the path to a friend's dorm.

If you do choose to try off-campus life, there is plenty of space available in the area. More than half of UM's student body lives off campus, so houses and apartments available for rent are fairly common in Coral Gables, South Miami, Kendall, and even up near downtown Miami. Traffic is certainly an issue no matter where you live, but you can cut down on problems by looking for a place right down the street in one of many neighborhoods within a mile of campus. Unfortunately, there are no neighborhoods that have been taken over by UM students as of yet, so you'll likely be living next to normal Miami families.

The College Prowler™ Grade on
Off-Campus
Housing: B+

A high grade in Off-Campus Housing indicates that apartments are of high quality, close to campus, affordable, and easy to secure.

Diversity

The Lowdown On...
Diversity

Asian or Pacific Islander:
7%

African American:
11%

Hispanic:
28%

White:
55%

American Indian:
0%

International:
7%

Unknown:
0%

Out of State:
40%

Most Popular Religions:
Religion isn't a major issue at UM, although there are plenty of clubs for more spiritual students on campus, regardless of their religions.

Political Activity

The student body seems more interested in going to the beach than protesting controversial political decisions. Although the city of Miami is known for its mixed political feelings, UM students don't seem to care much.

Gay Tolerance

Miami is famous for its wide-spread homosexual culture, especially in the South Beach area. Citizens are very accepting of the gay community, and UM mirrors that tolerance with organizations like spectrUM.

Economic Status

Given the high cost of attending UM and the fancy clothing seen around campus, many students seem to come from wealthy homes. This doesn't mean that there aren't plenty of students with modest backgrounds, but those really struggling with finances may want to consider a public university.

Minority Clubs

Minority students will feel right at home in the diverse atmosphere of Miami. Clubs like OASIS, Asian American Students Association, and African Students Union will help students meet others from their ethnic background.

Students Speak Out On...
Diversity

> "I read somewhere that we have one of the most diverse campuses in the United States, and that's evident from just walking around campus for a short amount of time."

Q "This school is called the global campus for a reason. **I have met fewer Americans than any other ethnicity.** I truly love that about this school."

Q "**We have a very diverse campus**. Over one hundred nations are represented. I actually chose this school because this was the only time in my life where I would have the chance to get to know so many people from so many different places"

Q "**There is no campus and no place on Earth more diverse than Miami**. It is the gateway to the international community. Sometimes it feels like English is the second language in this city."

Q "**Every style of person is represented here.** I believe there is someone from every state at least in the school, if not in my class level."

Q "The campus is very diverse. **There are people from many ethnic backgrounds**, as well as a lot of international students."

Q "There are **a lot of Hispanic people** here. But there's also a good mix of other cultures."

Q "**There are many different kinds of people on campus.**
There are also many international students."

Q "**UM consistently ranks among the top five schools in
the United States for the amount of diversity within its
student body**. It is one of the greatest things about the
university, knowing that I will be able to meet, talk to, and
learn with people from all around the country, as well as
the world. Each person makes the school more unique."

Q "**Our campus sucks when it comes to diversity.** There
are not many other ethnic groups other than white and
Hispanic."

The College Prowler Take On...
Diversity

Like most big cities, Miami has areas that are very cultural, and visiting these areas might feel like stepping into another world. Instead of Chinatown, Miami has Little Havana, the world's largest collection of Cubans outside of Cuba. The huge Hispanic population in Miami is not limited to one area. You'll overhear conversations spoken in Spanish almost everywhere in the city, and sometimes the accents are hard to understand and you end up with totally preposterous things in your McDonalds bag after an unsuccessful trip to the drive-thru. Most students get accustomed to Miami's Hispanic heritage pretty quickly and take advantage of the great atmosphere of Calle Ocho, the street that runs through the heart of Little Havana.

Miami has so many different ethnicities represented that students coming from non-diverse backgrounds may feel uncomfortable at first. As the numbers prove, only half of the students in most classes will be white. This is a great experience for students of any ethnicity. It basically forces you to understand different cultures and people from various backgrounds. It's especially interesting to hear what students from other countries write in English class when culture plays a major part. There are also many various religions represented. Christian clubs are popular, as are other religious organizations like Hillel. Homosexual students will also feel right at home, especially in South Beach, a hotspot for gay culture. Don't come to Miami expecting to be surrounded by the same people you would at a school in Iowa. According to U.S. News & World Report, UM is one of the most diverse campuses in the nation. Some students find this to be the best thing about life in Miami.

The College Prowler™ Grade on

Diversity: A-

A high grade in Diversity indicates that ethnic minorities and international students have a notable presence on campus and that students of different economic backgrounds, religious beliefs, and sexual preferences are well-represented.

Guys & Girls

The Lowdown On...
Guys & Girls

Men Undergrads:
42%

Women Undergrads:
58%

Birth Control Available?

Condoms are always available for free in a basket at the Student Health Center, and there are conferences and campaigns to promote awareness of teen pregnancy and birth control methods

Social Scene:

The school is very social and most guys and girls don't have trouble meeting people if they want to. Since almost all freshman live in the "Towers" their first year, they will often meet other students on their floor when they share bathroom facilities. Usually guys and girls live on alternate floors, so the opposite sex is never too far away. Since most students come to UM looking to make friends, it's never hard to find someone to hang out with, even if it takes a couple weeks to build stronger friendships.

Hookups or Relationships?

As is expected, most freshmen come to school without being in relationships. Random hookups are common in the beginning, but after a few months or a year, relationships take over. Miami is a great town for dating, with plenty of romantic spots and restaurants.

Best Place to Meet Guys/Girls:

The easiest way to meet a guy or girl for a quick hookup is at one of many clubs in Coconut Grove or at South Beach. Relationships are usually forged from neighbors, friends of friends, classmates, or study partners. If you're looking for a good view, wander out to the IM fields or the lawn around the lake, where students lay under the sun on blankets to read or study. The Rat is also a popular meeting place, as well as the fraternity houses or sorority suites.

If you're more into parties and less into dating, keep an eye out for house parties on the weekends and sometimes during the week. Fraternities sometimes throw big parties at their houses, but the better ones are off campus where they don't have to follow school rules. To get more involved in the non-UM party scene, you can always stop by one of the many bars or clubs in the Grove or mingle with the ultra-trendy South Beach crowd.

Did You Know?

Top Places to Find Hotties:

1. Any beach in Miami

2. Campus swimming pool

3. The Rat

Top Places to Hookup:

1. South Beach

2. Bars or clubs in Coconut Grove

3. House parties

4. Fraternities/Sororities

5. Co-Ed Dorms

Dress Code

The clothing seen on campus is almost as diverse as the students that go here. For every guy that falls out of bed five minutes before class and throws on sandals and jeans, there's a girl wearing the latest fashions to her math lectures. For daily life, pretty much anything goes. Most of the guys stick with shorts and t-shirts during the day, and the girls wear jeans and tank tops. Bring some preppy clothes for going out at night, when the standard dress is slacks and formal shirts for guys, and skirts and nice tops for girls. The heaviest thing you'll need as far as the weather goes is a hooded sweatshirt and jeans. Make sure to bring a comfortable pair of sandals, a UM staple for both guys and girls.

Students Speak Out On...
Guys & Girls

{ **"Every type of person is represented here. We have nerds, jerks, punks, rockers, everything."**

Q "**The girls are awesome...looking**. That's about all I can say"

Q "**The girls are amazing.** They are all beautiful, but the question is if it's on the inside or just outer beauty. The friends I have made have generally not been supermodels, but quality girls, and I leave the models for just looking because I know at this campus the girls can be a little rude, but truly worth a try."

Q "**The guys are short like me** for the most part, unlike a northern school where the shortest guy is six feet tall."

Q "The girls are awesome. **Watch out for personality**. Some girls in Miami lack it! But beauty is definitely not a problem."

Q "**People here are interesting.** A lot of Eastern attitude comes out, in my opinion. As a Midwesterner I am used to a little more hospitality. However, I do believe that this is no different from any other campus."

Q "**The girls are incredible.** There is no hotter place on earth than here, with beautiful women from all over the world that sometimes have the attitude to go with it. I must say, that is on the negative side. I have many friends and I simply believe that it is about finding your comfort zone. The same sort of people are looking for the type of friends that they are used to from back home, or a group that suits their needs. I think it is important to find your niche and you will be happy. I found mine in a fraternity and have been loving it since."

The College Prowler Take On...
Guys & Girls

The opinion of most UM students seems to be that the student body's bodies are great to look at, but that this is not a school to meet your future spouse. Temporary flings or random hooking up is common among freshmen who are basking in their post-high school freedom. But once everyone gets settled and makes the friends they'll have for the next four years, relationships kick in. There are plenty of great places around Miami to take a date, as far as restaurants and nightspots go. But finding someone on campus who fulfills your emotional needs as well as your physical ones might prove challenging. Perhaps the biggest problem is that guys and girls hide their real identities in favor of tight clothes and good tans, since that seems to be the look most students are going for.

The school can be as promiscuous as you want it to be. If you're looking for a quick hook up, it's not hard to head to a bar or club. Most students don't make this a habit, as it obviously complicates things a great deal. Your best bet is to make a bunch of friends that are the opposite sex in the beginning of your freshman year, and then you'll have plenty of connections to guys or girls for the rest of college. Overall, the guys and girls look great, and, to be fair, some are great all around. But the amount of really intelligent, nice, caring people who are also hot seems to be low. Many other colleges face the opposite situation, so you have to ask yourself if you're looking for long-term relationships in college or if you just want to have some fun with no commitment.

The College Prowler™ Grade on
Guys: B+

A high grade for Guys indicates that the male population on campus is attractive, smart, friendly, and engaging, and that the school has a decent ratio of guys to girls.

The College Prowler™ Grade on
Girls: A-

A high grade for Girls not only implies that the women on campus are attractive, smart, friendly, and engaging, but also that there is a fair ratio of girls to guys.

Athletics

The Lowdown On...
Athletics

Athletic Division:
Division I

Conference:
Atlantic Coast Conference

Men's Varsity Sports:
Basketball
Baseball
Cross Country
Football
Track & Field
Tennis
Swimming & Diving

Women's Varsity Sports:
Basketball
Golf
Cross Country
Track & Field
Soccer
Rowing
Swimming & Diving
Tennis
Volleyball

→

Club Sports:

Badminton
Baseball
Bowling
Golf
Karate
Lacrosse
PHATE (Promoting Health Awareness Through Education)
Racquetball
Roller Hockey
Rowing
Rugby
Sailing
SCUBA
Soccer
Squash
Swimming
Tennis
Ultimate Frisbee
Volleyball
Water Polo

Intramurals:

Arena Football
Basketball
Dodgeball
Fantasy Football
Flag Football
Floor Hockey
Golf
Indoor Soccer
Innertube Water Polo
Kickball
Soccer
Softball
Team Billiards
Team Racquetball
Tennis Singles
Ultimate Frisbee
Volleyball
Wallyball
Whiffle Ball

Athletic Fields

IM Field

Orange Bowl (Football)

Convocation Center (Basketball)

Mark Light Stadium (Baseball)

School Mascot

Sebastion the Ibis

Getting Tickets

Attending UM is a sports-lover's dream. Students get free access to any UM sporting event with their ID card. Tickets to football bowl games are also available for students to purchase, and the school puts together packages to get students to attend away games during football season. The basketball arena and baseball stadium on campus are fun places to see a game for free.

Most Popular Sports

There's no questioning what the most popular sport is on campus. Football dominates every weekend during the season, with students donating their Saturday afternoons to supporting the team. It also helps to have a program that's continually ranked among the top in the country. The baseball team is also one of the country's best, but doesn't get nearly the amount of attention the football team does. Other sports are very competitive in their divisions, but don't get the student support they likely deserve.

Best Place to Take a Walk

The path around the lake or the road that circles the school.

Overlooked Teams

The women's basketball team is among the top in its division and even in the country, but few pay attention to it. The baseball team gets great recognition nationally, but you're more likely to see Sportscenter anchors talking about it than you are to hear it in a conversation among students.

Gyms/Facilities

Wellness Center

This huge gym is one of the campus's best attributes. The machines and facilities are state-of-the-art, and the indoor swimming pool and hot tub are a hit with students. Beyond that, there are plenty of racquetball and squash courts, indoor and outdoor basketball courts, and a juice bar. The Wellness Center stays open until midnight on weeknights, 11 p.m. on Friday, and 10 p.m. on Saturday and Sunday.

Students Speak Out On...
Athletics

"Football is huge, since we have one of the best teams in the nation, and basketball is getting there. IM sports are also huge, with large programs occurring each spring and fall semester."

Q "**Athletics are an essential part of on campus life.** Sports Fest is great fun and you really connect with your teammates. It's definitely worth doing IM sports if you are into it."

Q "**Varsity football and basketball are very popular on campus.** Everyone goes to the football games and over half of the students attend the basketball games. IM sports are also very popular. Many people participate in IM football, soccer, racquetball, etc."

Q "Miami is one of the nation's leading sports programs. **There is nothing like Hurricane Football** and the history that comes with it. I am a huge sports fan and one of the main draws was coming to watch the sports here. Although the basketball team is not necessarily all I wished it to be, they have a brand new facility on campus which makes it convenient to go to games, unlike the Orange Bowl which is located in a shady area of town."

Q "**Intramurals are as big as you want them to be.** They are well formed and have a place just to organize and get together. I am the IM chair for my fraternity and am a huge supporter of IM's on campus. They are really competitive and well officiated. They offer flag indoor and outdoor football, basketball, dodgeball, kickball, water polo, indoor and outdoor soccer, softball, tennis, and many others. It is definitely a great program."

Q "This is the University of Miami. Do you really have to ask about varsity sports? As far as IM sports go, **there is always a tournament in something going on**."

Q "**Varsity sports are huge on campus,** mainly football and baseball, and basketball is growing. IM sports are very prevalent, particularly for fraternities. Arena football, flag football, and basketball are some of the more popular ones."

Q "**Sports are really big on campus,** especially with National Championship football and baseball. IM sports are big when spring comes around."

Q "**Everyone goes to the football games**, obviously. The new Convocation Center is nice, so some people go to basketball games too."

Q "**It seems like varsity football is the only thing that matters here.** Basketball and baseball are just fillers until the football season, even though we have an excellent baseball team. IM football and basketball are very big. Tennis and golf are also popular."

The College Prowler Take On...
Athletics

Although UM students might be lazy when it comes to academics, politics, or national events, one thing they take seriously is football. It helps, of course, that UM has one of the most dominant college football programs in the country, and that the team shows no sign of dropping out of the nation's top tier. A true sign of a college student's devotion is how early they're willing to wake up. For noon games on Saturdays, students line up outside the Orange Bowl gates as early as 8 a.m. to ensure good seats. By the mid morning, the lines wind out into the parking lot, and the massive student section of the Orange Bowl is generally buzzing. This is especially true for the big games against rivals like the University of Florida or Florida State University. Tickets to every UM sport are free to students, but not many people bother with anything but football, even though we have a perennial National Championship contender in our baseball team.

Intramurals also play a big part in campus life. There's a yearly competition between the residential colleges called Sportsfest, where teams from the dorms compete in dozens of games over a weekend. There are also intramurals during the fall and the spring, where the activity is dominated by fraternities, but can also include various other organizations. The IM games get pretty heated, especially in popular sports like flag football and basketball. Most students seem happy with the extensive intramurals and the excellent facilities on the massive, well-lit IM field. Sportsfest is a fun way to compete against other dorms and other floors from within your building, and it also helps to build bonds between floormates. But the most important thing will always be the football team, proven by the funeral-like silence the day after any rare loss.

The College Prowler™ Grade on

Athletics: A

A high grade in Athletics indicates that students have school spirit, that sports programs are respected, that games are well-attended, and that intramurals are a prominent part of student life.

Nightlife

The Lowdown On...
Nightlife

Club and Bar Prowler:
Popular Nightlife Spots!

Club Prowler:

Clubs are a big part of college life, and there's no better place for them than Miami. Coconut Grove is popular among the college crowd, especially on Thursday nights. If you're feeling more adventurous, take a 20-minute trip to South Beach, arguably the hottest club scene in the world. Here are the spots you shouldn't miss in Miami.

Crobar

1445 Washington Ave.
South Beach
(305) 531-8225
www.crobarmiami.com

Crobar is one of the more popular clubs in South Beach, but it's not really considered one of the best. Its location on a crowded corner in the heart of SoBe certainly adds to its popularity, but the majority of students seem to try Crobar once and settle into some lesser known, yet nicer, South Beach nightspot.

B.E.D.
929 Washington Ave.
South Beach
(305) 532-9070
www.bedmiami.com

B.E.D. is a rare example of when a theme-reliant club succeeds. Although this club is fairly young, it has grown to be one of the top spots in South Beach, due largely to the innovative idea of serving patrons dinner not at tables or chairs, but in bed. If you don't come with enough people, you might have to share your bed with another party, which isn't always a bad thing. Ordering from the fancy menu is mandatory upon entry, and food alone can cost you $50, not including the drink minimums.

Sunday: Closed

Monday: "Secret Society Dinner Party" Women eat free, RSVP required.

Thursday: "Disco Jazz Night" Free admission for everyone, and one complimentary drink if you bring a girl.

Friday: "Abstrakt Fridays"

Saturday: "Dressed Party"

Nikki Beach
1 Ocean Dr.
South Beach
(305) 538-1111
www.nikkibeach.com

This outdoor beach club is a refreshing alternative to the crowded, sweaty dark rooms featured in other clubs. Nikki Beach is a cross between club and resort. The partying literally never stops, as you can always find people out in the mornings and afternoons, enjoying cocktails and the sights of the beautiful people around them. This spot is considered one of the most exclusive clubs in Miami, so entry will probably be denied to most college students; those who get in never want to leave. This club has more of a tourist and visitor crowd, because anyone who lived this 24-hour hedonistic lifestyle for more than a couple days would probably get burnt out pretty quickly.

Thursday: "Retro 80's"

Friday: "Tangerine Dreams"

Saturday: "Winter in Miami"

Sunday: Brunch from 10 a.m.-2 p.m. then "Indio Loco" at night

Oxygen

2911 Grand Ave.
Coconut Grove
Subterranean Level
Streets of Mayfair
(305) 476-0202
www.oxygenlounge.biz

Although the club scene in Coconut Grove comes nowhere close to South Beach, this underground club has become popular with students looking to stay closer to campus. Oxygen's upscale sushi menu and cool location below ground in the Grove adds to its charm, but more serious clubbers will find this to be a weak spot compared to the craziness of South Beach. Part of this is intentional, as Oxygen promotes itself as a quieter lounge-type atmosphere instead of a noisy club.

Friday: "Vive Fridays"

Saturday: "Escape Saturdays"

Opium

136 Collins Ave.
South Beach
(305) 531-5535
www.opiummiami.com

Yet another South Beach hotspot, Opium competes mainly with clubs like Crobar, Space, Level, and the tons of other popular places. Opium advertises a lot with fliers around campus, and so it appears to be more popular at first glance. Opium is one of the big-name clubs, like Crobar, that everyone has to try once, but most people end up going to a smaller spot.

Bar Prowler:

For those not into blinding lights and techno music, you'll find a better atmosphere in one of the many bars in Coconut Grove. Check out some of these student favorites:f

Monty's

2550 S. Bayshore Dr.
Coconut Grove
(305) 858-1431
www.montysstonecrab.com

Monty's is a tough sell for those who've never been there. The location, although in the Grove, is pretty far removed from the heart of the bar scene. The most popular area is out on the deck by the water, which clashes with the dark, smoky atmosphere of most of the local drinking spots. But Monty's is one of the hottest locales for early evening drinking, especially with mixed drinks like the Painkiller. This isn't really a late night hangout, so there aren't many specials or theme nights, but few weekends go by without gathering on the deck at Monty's for "pre-gaming".

Mr. Moe's

3131 Commodore Plaza
Coconut Grove
(305) 442-1114
www.mrmoes.com

Mr. Moe's has a pretty cool log cabin décor and the attitude to match. Wednesday nights

Mr. Moe's (*Continued...*)

are especially interesting with a bull riding theme, and Karaoke night on Tuesdays is always fun. Like a lot of other bars, Mr. Moe's has happy hour every night before 8 p.m., and features a ton of TV's for sporting events. The food is actually pretty good, and fairly cheap for the Grove, and so the place stays open as a restaurant during the day before turning into the typical bar at night, with a mid-western slant.

Sandbar

3064 Grand Ave.
Coconut Grove
(305) 444-5270
www.sandbargrill.com

Sandbar, is a top destination for UM students looking to drink and have a good time without the hectic pace of a club in South Beach. For the most part a bar is a bar, but Sandbar stays popular because of its specials and theme nights. The White Trash Bash every Tuesday is a fun theme for students with hokey trailer park attire on hand. The biggest weeknight for a college bar is of course Thursday, so Sandbar offers $3 bottles and a special late-night happy hour from 2 a.m.-5 a.m. with $2 bottles. Other specials include Aloha Fridays and half price tacos on Mondays.

The Tavern

3416 Main Hwy.
Coconut Grove
(305) 447-3884
www.tavernmiami.com

This favorite of UM students is known for its cheap drinks, generous specials, and fairly lenient ID checking. There's a happy hour every weeknight before 8 p.m., but the best special is all-you-can-drink on Monday nights for $10. Other nights basically feature various beers at cheap prices, except for Sunday night, when the combination of $5 pitchers and beer pong ensures an interesting evening.

Titanic

5813 Ponce De Leon Blvd.
Coral Gables
(305) 667-2537
www.titanicbrewery.com

Titanic is rare for a Miami bar in that it's not in the Grove or South Beach. But this spot became popular because of its location right next to campus, and because it's the only bar within reasonable walking distance of UM. It has become popular with the UM crowd because of its great live music, relaxed atmosphere, and lack of a cover charge. Titanic brews its own beer, some of which it names after UM traditions, and there are plenty of specials and happy hour drinks. With no cover charge and no minimum age for entry, it won't hurt to walk down the street and give Titanic a try.

Other Places to Check Out:

Deep, Life, Tobacco Road, Fat Tuesday's, Senor Frog's, Delano, Level, Space, Wet Willie's, Quench

Bars Close At:

3 a.m.

Primary Areas with Nightlife:

Coconut Grove, South Beach

Cheapest Place to Get a Drink:

The Tavern

Student Favorites

Monty's, The Tavern, Sandbar, Mr. Moe's, Senor Frog's, Crobar, Oxygen, Titanic, Opium

Favorite Drinking Games:

Beer Pong

Card Games

Century Club

Quarters

Power Hour

Useful Resources for Nightlife

www.cityvibz.com/miami/miamiclubs.shtml

The Miami New Times

Street Magazine

What to Do if You're Not 21

Café Demetrio

300 Alhambra Circle
Coral Gables
(305) 448-4949
www.cafedemetrio.com

Although you won't find wild dancing and barely dressed hotties at this coffeehouse, Café Demetrio provides a quiet but cool atmosphere for students who prefer coffee and a good book to blaring techno tunes and fake IDs. This quaint coffee bar in downtown Coral Gables is popular among the artsy crowd, and brings in live bands to spice things up on Friday and Saturday night. There's even a chess tournament night on the first Monday of every month. Make sure to check out the gourmet coffee and snacks at this local landmark.

Books and Books

265 Aragon Ave.
Coral Gables
(305) 442-4408www.booksandbooks.com

Okay, so hanging out at a book store probably doesn't appeal to the bar and club crowd, but if you're into art or writing or poetry, then you'll want to make Books and Books a priority. This 20-year-old independent bookstore was a hit with locals long before Barnes and Noble became a nationally recognized name. The location in beautiful downtown Coral Gables has hosted an incredible list of celebrity authors and poets like Martin Ames, Allen Ginsburg, Jamaica Kincaid, Salman Rushdie, Kurt Vonnegut, Judy Blume, Walter Cronkite, Dave Barry, Carl Hiaasen, Jimmy Carter, Al Gore, Rudy Giuliani, Rosie O'Donnell, Cindy Crawford, and Mariel Hemingway. The store keeps a pretty up-to-date listing of upcoming readings and events on their website, so be sure to check and see if anyone cool is coming soon. Books and Books also looks to entertain its loyal patrons with live music and a nice café.

House Parties:

The house parties in Miami are not as popular as those at other colleges because of the competition provided by local clubs and bars. But there are still usually a few worthy parties every weekend on Ponce (the street bordering campus) or in the local neighborhoods where many off-campus students live

Organization Parties:

The only organizations throwing popular parties around campus are the fraternities, who host events at their houses on occasion. If there are other parties, you'll find a flyer on your windshield, under the door of your room, or jammed into the side of your car. The only other groups who would even think about trying to compete with the clubs and bars in the area are the school newspaper and radio station, who sometimes partner to sponsor house parties.

Students Speak Out On...
Nightlife

"Well, after encountering parties on campus, I would say they are amazing, especially the ones in the apartment areas. Just make sure you aren't underage when you drink in this city because they are pretty strict about ID's."

Q "**The parties on campus are typically kept dry and 'unexciting**.' Parties off campus (of which there are many every weekend) are more alcoholic and wild in nature."

Q "Some great bars in the Grove are Sandbar, Mr. Moe's, and the Tavern, and on South Beach I would have to go with **Nikki Beach and Opium**."

Q "**Parties on campus are decent, but the off campus parties are better.** You simply have to ask around 8 p.m. that night to find out where the parties are and then crash them."

Q "Parties do not really happen on campus because the RAs and on campus police are a little strict. However, **the off campus parties are pretty good.** I choose to go to places where I know most of the people there, but that is just a preference. The city is full of bars, but for the most part students stick around Coconut Grove. This is the college bar scene located about ten minutes from campus. It features such bars as Wet Willies, Monty's, and Sandbar, but for a lot of these places you need to be of age or have a good fake."

Q "**The parties at UM range from mediocre to decent.**
Coral Gables police are always on the prowl. Fortunately, there are a multitude of excellent bars and clubs nearby (too many to name, in fact)."

Q "**Parties on campus are rarities, being mainly dry.**
Bars and clubs are very well represented in South Beach and Coconut Grove, with reputable names like Oxygen, Crobar, and Tobacco Road."

Q "The parties on campus are alright, although **most of the stuff on frat row seems to be under the watchful eye of the dean's office** and the Coral Gables Police Department. As far as bars and stuff, Crobar and Tavern are good places with lots of UM students. Then there are of course the nice clubs on South Beach."

The College Prowler Take On...
Nightlife

If you have any interest in coming to Miami for college, you've probably already heard about the nightlife. Celebrities flock to South Beach every weekend to party at some of the hottest clubs in the world, with UM students dancing by their sides. The Miami area has two primary areas for nightlife. First, there's Coconut Grove, which is mostly composed of shops, restaurants, and bars, and is about a 10 minute drive from campus. Most of the popular bars students attend are located here. Truly serious partiers will head to the clubs and 24-hour party atmosphere of South Beach, one of Miami's most famous cultural areas and a fixture in the nightlife scene of South Florida.

There are other, quieter bars around campus, but to say you're "going out" at UM generally means either SoBe or the Grove. Attire for South Beach is usually pretty chic, depending on the theme of the club you're hitting up. For the bars in the Grove, dress however you feel. There are some great drink specials in the Grove, and it doesn't take long to hear from friends which spots are carding and which don't mind a decent fake ID. South Beach is absurdly expensive, which reflects the ritzy crowd it attracts nightly. You'll want at least a few $20s whenever you head to South Beach, and that may only get you in the door and a couple of overpriced drinks. If you figure out when the specials and happy hours are in the Grove, you can make a few bucks go a long way. The bars in the Grove are most popular on weekends and Thursday nights, but South Beach never slows down. As far as other parties go, most are outshined by the excellent spots around town, but there are usually a few house parties just outside campus that survive.

The College Prowler™ Grade on

Nightlife: A+

A high grade in Nightlife indicates that there are many bars and clubs in the area that are easily accessible and affordable. Other determining factors include the number of options for the under-21 crowd and the prevalence of house parties.

Greek Life

The Lowdown On...
Greek Life

Number of Fraternities:
10

Number of Sororities:
7

Percent of Undergrad Men in Fraternities:
12%

Percent of Undergrad Women in Sororities:
12%

Fraternities on Campus:
Alpha Sigma Phi
Kappa Sigma
Lambda Chi Alpha
Phi Delta Theta
Pi Kappa Alpha
Sigma Alpha Epsilon
Sigma Alpha Mu
Sigma Chi
Sigma Phi Epsilon
Zeta Beta Tau

➡

Sororities on Campus:

Delta Delta Delta
Delta Gamma
Delta Phi Epsilon
Kappa Kappa Gamma
Sigma Delta Tau
Zeta Tau Alpha
Alpha Delta Pi

Other Greek Organizations:

Association of Greek Letter Organizations
Interfraternity Council
Latino Greek Council
National Panhellenic Council
Alpha Lambda Delta
Gamma Sigma Alpha
Omicron Delta Kappa
Order of Omega
Rho Lambda

Multicultural Colonies:

Lambda Theta Alpha
Phi Iota Alpha
Alpha Kappa Alpha
Alpha Phi Alpha
Kappa Alpha Psi
Omega Psi Phi
Phi Beta Sigma
Sigma Gamma Rho
Zeta Phi Beta

Did You Know?

Most UM fraternities and sororities participate in two major competitions per year. In the fall, there's Homecoming, when the organizations battle for victory by **attending volunteer events**, building floats, and staging skits called Organized Cheer. The big event of the spring is Greek Week, when similar events are held, along with more sports-oriented games and contests.

The 12% of students who are Greek hold **85% of the campus leadership positions**.

UM has **a very strict anti-hazing policy** and monitors all Greek organizations during every rush and pledge period.

Students Speak Out On...
Greek Life

"As I am a member of the Greek community, I can say that Greek life is very interesting. It gives you the chance to meet so many new people, and find out things about yourself that you never would have otherwise. Only about 11% of the campus is Greek, so there is no raw dominance by the Greeks on campus."

"**Greek life is a lot of fun** and I would recommend that everyone check out the fraternities and sororities represented on campus. Fraternities do throw parties often, but unfortunately people usually go to non-Greek sponsored parties."

"**Greek Life is definitely not a dominating scene** on this campus, since the percentage is only about 12% of students. However, I am a member of the Greek community and I'm loving the fraternity I am in. All of my friends are members of the fraternity and/or sorority scene."

"I waited a semester before joining, since for fraternities there is both fall and spring rush, and found the right fraternity for me. I believe that it was the best move to figure out what each fraternity stands for. **It is also a very good way to meet people**, as well as the opposite sex. There are different fraternities or sororities, and each has something to offer according to what you are looking for."

Q "**Greek life does not dominate the social scene**, which is good in that it forces the fraternities and sororities to have higher standards. In general though, most of the Greek organizations are involved in their own activities and do not interact with the rest of the student body."

Q "**Greek life is only a fraction of the campus,** but everything done socially either has their name on it officially or unofficially. The social level of the campus does rest on the Greek's shoulders, being that if it's doing poorly the Greeks are to blame.'"

Q "**Greek life keeps you busy** and allows for a lot of interaction and meeting of new people. It is definitely one of the best ways to break into student government and has many positive attributes."

The College Prowler Take On...
Greek Life

Greek Life is not a disruptive force on campus, but it is sizeable enough to make a difference. Although UM does not have the massive Greek system in place at some universities, there are plenty of fraternities and sororities for students to choose from. If you want to stay away from Greek life, you won't have to try hard at UM. The fraternity houses are lined on a road on the edge of campus, and the sorority and fraternity suites are in a building in a quiet part of UM. If not for the letter shirts seen around school, non-Greek students could easily forget that there are even fraternities and sororities at UM. But behind the scenes, the Greek system here is very important. Although only 12% of UM's population is Greek, 85% of the leadership positions on campus are held by members of fraternities and sororities.

The social aspect of Greek life is present at UM, but is not overwhelming. The fraternities host parties occasionally at their houses, but UM's real social scene can be found at the bars and clubs in Miami. For the most part, Greeks hang out with other Greeks. The fraternities and sororities compete against each other in intramurals and Homecoming events, as well as a yearly competition called Greek Week. There is certainly a bond that exists between members of the Greek community, as well as a strong sense of pride and competition with other Greek organizations. If you've been studying episodes of MTV's Fraternity Life in preparation for college, you may want to look elsewhere. But if you want a Greek system that is quiet but still important, you will like UM's.

The College Prowler™ Grade on
Greek Life: B+

A high grade in Greek Life indicates that sororities and fraternities are not only present, but also active on campus. Other determining factors include the variety of houses available and the respect the Greek community receives from the rest of the campus.

Drug Scene

The Lowdown On...
Drug Scene

Most Prevalent Drugs on Campus:

Alcohol
Marijuana
Ecstasy
Cocaine

Liquor-Related Discipline Cases:
234

Liquor-Related Arrests:
0

Drug-Related Discipline Cases:
20

Drug-Related Arrests:
4

Drug Counseling Programs

PIER21
Phone: (305) 284-6120
Services: alcohol and drug education, prevention, and intervention

Student Counseling Center
Phone: (305) 284-5511

Services: general psychological counseling service, referrals to specialized counseling

BACCHUS (Boosting Alcohol Consciousness Concerning the Health of University Students)
Services: alcohol education in regards to college students

Students Speak Out On...
Drug Scene

> "I can honestly say that I have never run into anyone attempting to buy, sell, or use drugs. I'm sure that they're out there, but I suppose they hide themselves very well."

Q "**I have not seen too many people doing drugs**. The handful of times I have witnessed someone doing drugs was at an off campus event and they were smoking marijuana."

Q "**In Miami, there are many drug problems** with such drugs as Ecstasy. However, I have not seen very much, as I have never been around or really been introduced to a drug beyond marijuana. I have been told there are pretty heavy drugs around, I just don't know what and where. It is definitely avoidable though.."

Q "**There is a drug problem on campus**. Many of the students are wealthy and think they have nothing better to spend daddy's money on than marijuana or crack, or alcohol for that matter."

Q "**Alcohol is very prevalent**, and definitely lives up to the stereotype of being everywhere on a college campus."

Q "**There is a lot of weed being smoked**, but anything more serious than that isn't very apparent."

Q "Drugs on college campuses will always be present. **Even though there have been efforts to prevent it, they are not effective.** Drug use is wrong and there should be more methods to stop it."

The College Prowler Take On...
Drug Scene

College mirrors reality in that if you want drugs, you can always find them. Miami, like any big city, has its fair share of bad neighborhoods and drug addicts. But it's easy to stay away from them, especially around the campus in upscale Coral Gables. The only drug being really abused on UM's campus is alcohol, and that's true of almost all colleges. There are groups of students that are into marijuana, cocaine, ecstasy, or various other drugs. But dealing is not really a problem on campus and most RAs are pretty strict about looking out for drug use in the dorms. Given UM's fairly difficult classes, most hardcore drug users aren't going to be around for long.

Most students don't seem worried about drugs on campus. While UM isn't going to make any top ten lists of schools with drug problems, there is certainly a dependency on alcohol at social events and in the lives of most students. Alcohol is most popular with incoming freshmen, who seem to feel the need to abuse it once they get away from their parents. It stays a force throughout college life, especially once you and your friends start turning 21. Most of the time, your exposure to drugs at school depends on who you makes friends with. It's not hard to get sucked into a circle of potheads if you let it happen, but if you want to say no, you won't have a problem. Turning down alcohol at UM can be more difficult, as it plays an extremely important part in most students' social lives.

The College Prowler™ Grade on

Drug Scene: B-

A high grade in the Drug Scene indicates that drugs are not a noticeable part of campus life; drug use is not visible, and no pressure to use them seems to exist.

Campus Strictness

The Lowdown On...
Campus Strictness

What Are You Most Likely to Get Caught Doing on Campus?

- Being publicly intoxicated
- Burning candles or incense in dorm rooms
- Downloading music on the school network
- Drinking underage
- Making too much noise in the dorms
- Not leaving the room during fire alarms
- Parking illegally or without a permit
- Playing hallway sports
- Setting off fire alarms
- Smoking indoors
- Stealing food from the dining halls

Students Speak Out On...
Campus Strictness

> "The police are generally pretty good. They look out for your welfare and don't arrest you unless you deserve it, which takes a lot of pushing the limits."

Q "**I haven't run into any situation** where police became involved."

Q "The University of Miami has its own police force, which is quite annoying. **I have never seen more meter maids in my life**. They sit in a golf cart and go around all day and all night giving tickets."

Q "There really are no on campus parties and you can only really get busted if you can't walk in without falling down past 10 p.m. **Parties are not permitted on campus,** but you can get around the police otherwise."

Q "**Campus police are very strict about some things**. They're always out patrolling fraternity row, ensuring safety and stopping underage drinking, much to the dismay of the students. Their presence is very noticeable."

Q "**Police bust more people on drinking** than on anything else."

Q "**I don't think the police are too strict.** I know people that have been caught doing drugs in the dorms that are still permitted to live there."

Q "I know a person who is related to a trustee who got **discovered with drugs in the dorms and nothing happened**."

The College Prowler Take On...
Campus Strictness

Students are quick to point out the presence of police officers on campus, especially late at night. This is a good thing as far as safety goes, but makes getting away with things a lot harder. Every floor of the residence halls has RAs who are trained to look out for drinking and other illicit activities. Some RAs are strict and will report you over anything, while others actually allow drinking as long as it doesn't get out of control. Either way, the RAs are usually pretty cool and are just trying to keep everyone safe. The campus police are strict, but they can't cover every corner of campus, so kids still get away with plenty of underage drinking, the most common infraction on campus. Students have to check in to the dorms whenever they return after 10 p.m., so if you come back totally drunk and unable to walk, you'll probably get written up for public intoxication. Normally the police won't be involved, but you'll have to meet with a counselor and your parents will find out.

One of the more annoying areas of strictness is with the parking lot police. These guys ride around on golf carts and write tickets for anyone double parked or parked in the wrong lot, or even people who park over the white lines on the ground, even if the guy next to you was the cause of it. Some parking citations are absolutely ridiculous, but they're easy to appeal as long as you don't get too many. The most common reason for getting in trouble on campus is definitely underage drinking in the dorms. If you get noise complaints and run around the halls, even the most lenient RAs are bound to get fed up and turn you in.

B

The College Prowler™ Grade on

**Campus
Strictness: B**

A high Campus Strictness grade implies an overall lenient atmosphere; police and RAs are fairly tolerant, and the administration's rules are flexible.

Parking

The Lowdown On...
Parking

Approximate Parking Permit Cost:
$200-$298 per year

UM Parking Services
(305) 284-3096
parking@miami.edu
http://www.miami.edu/parking

Student Parking Lot?
Yes

Common Parking Tickets:
Expired Meter: $20
No Parking Zone: $20
Handicapped Zone: $250
Fire Lane: $20 + automatic towing & additional charges from Coral Gables police

Freshman Allowed to Park?
Yes.

Parking Permits

Permits are relatively easy to get if you apply within the first couple days of the year. You can apply on the school's network and the amount will be added to your bill automatically. You'll then have to go to the office in one of the garages on campus and pick up your permit, which hangs from your mirror and allows you access to almost all the lots on campus.

Did You Know?

Best Places to Find a Parking Spot

Apartment Area Lot, Ponce Garage

Pavia Garage, Mahoney/Pearson Garage

Convocation Center Lot, Anywhere on weekends and Friday or Saturday night

Good Luck Getting a Parking Spot Here!

Hecht/Stanford Lot

School Building and Classroom Lots (during the day)

Mahoney/Pearson Lot

Eaton Lot

Students Speak Out On...
Parking

"If you have a small car, it's easy. If not, it's challenging. Take early classes, because as the day goes by, it's harder to park. Once you find a legal spot keep your car there. This year they have ample room, so it's been nice."

Q "I do not have a car on campus, however I have many friends who do, and for them, **parking is typically a nightmare.** If you know when not to leave, it is typically not a problem, but with an increasing amount of freshman bringing cars every year, parking is becoming a bigger issue."

Q "I park in the Ponce de Leon Garage. I have never had a problem parking there. Commuter students, on the other hand, complain about parking. Parking in the lots located on campus could be difficult, but **there is always room in one of the three garages** located on campus."

Q "**Parking can get really annoying**. If you do not have a parking permit and try to park, you will be victim of the meter maid brigade. My brother commutes and says that if you do not get early to class you can have a terrible time parking. If you live on campus there is always a place to park, it is just how close you are to your building."

Q "Early morning and evenings are fine, but do not expect to get a good spot between those hours. **The school sells a lot more permits than they have spots**."

Q "**The parking scene is horrible.** Most students on campus seem to have a car and so parking spots are hard to come by. Parking on weekends is sometimes easier as many local students go home for the weekend."

Q "**Parking is crazy**. Depending on where you live or where you want to park your car, it can be very difficult."

Q "It seems that for an on campus student, parking is not much of a problem. However, **for commuter students, it is a severe issue.** Either you will have to walk or take the shuttle from the garage and kill a bunch of time. Or you might have to park in the commuter lots and hope nothing happens to your car (scratches, dents, etc)."

The College Prowler Take On...
Parking

The good news about parking at UM is that decals are available for freshmen. The bad news is that Braveheart-like battle scenes erupt over every decent spot available. There are tons of spots in the lots and garages around campus, so if you can cover the ever-increasing cost of a decal ($298 for the 2003/2004 year), then you're guaranteed to find a place to park. But finding a spot within reasonable walking distance to your dorm is another story. The two dorms where most freshmen live share a long, narrow lot with most of the good spots reserved for RA's and other staff. If you get back to campus in the popular parking times, which seem to be almost always, then your only hope of getting anything in this lot is to beg strangers for their spots. Instead, you'll probably have to park at UM's basketball arena and drag your stuff down the street to the building you live in.

Other dorms on campus have similar parking problems. Finding a good spot is an accomplishment worthy of celebration, and whenever you do hit the parking lot jackpot, you'll be reluctant to move your car for days, or even weeks. Still, it's better to put up with the occasional long walk than to not be allowed to have a car at all as a freshman, a policy which is becoming popular among today's overcrowded schools. Miami is a great city, but without a car, you'll be stuck eating at the same few restaurants and going to same places around campus. If you bring a car to school, make sure to get your decal early and try not to return to campus during weekday afternoons or mornings, when spots are rare. Evenings and weekends, when a lot of people leave campus, are the best times to find a place to park, but even then you should be prepared to walk.

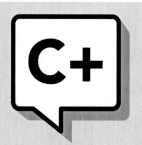

The College Prowler™ Grade on

Parking: C+

A high grade in this section indicates that parking is both available and affordable, and that parking enforcement isn't overly severe.

Transportation

The Lowdown On...
Transportation

Ways to Get Around Town
On Campus

Hurry 'Cane Shuttle
7 a.m.-10 p.m.
(305) 284-3096

RSMAS Shuttle
7:45 a.m.-5:30 p.m. weekdays,
(305) 284-3096

Sergeant Sebastian Escort,
6 p.m.-12 a.m.
After 12 a.m. by request
(305) 284-6666

Ibis Ride
8 p.m.-3:30 a.m.
Friday-Saturday
(305) 284-3096

Public Transportation
Metrorail, elevated train
system with a stop at UM

Taxi Cabs
Central Taxicab Service
(305) 532-5555

Diamond Cab Co.
(305) 545-5555

Flamingo Taxi
(305) 759-8100

Metro Taxi
(305) 888-8888

Society Cab Co.
(305) 757-5523

→

Super Yellow Cab Co.
(305) 888-7777

Tropical Taxicab Co.
(305) 945-1025

Yellow Cab Co.
(305) 633-0503

Car Rentals

Alamo, local: (305) 633-6076
national: (800) 327-9633
www.alamo.com

Avis

local: (305) 341-0936
national: (800) 831-2847
www.avis.com

Budget
national: (800) 527-0700
www.budget.com

Dollar
local: (305) 894-5068
national: (800) 800-4000.
www.dollar.com

Enterprise
local: (305) 447-0308
national: (800) 736-8222
www.enterprise.com

Hertz
local: (305) 223-2000
national: (800) 654-3131
www.hertz.com

Best Ways to Get Around Town

Your best friend's car

A bike (wear a helmet, this is Miami)

Ways to Get Out of Town

Airlines Serving Miami:

American Airlines
(800) 433-7300
www.americanairlines.com

Continental
(800) 523-3273
www.continental.com

Delta
(800) 221-1212
www.delta-air.com

Northwest
(800) 225-2525
www.nwa.com

United
(800) 241-6522
www.united.com

US Airways
(800) 428-4322
www.usairways.com

Airport

Miami International Airport
(305) 876-7000

The Miami International Airport is seven miles and approximately 20 minutes driving time from the University of Miami

How to Get to the Airport

Super Shuttle International, (305) 871-2000. The van will pick you up in front of your dorm and take you to your terminal at MIA.

A Cab Ride to the Airport Costs: $18

Greyhound

The Greyhound Bus Station is near the Miami International Airport, approximately seven miles from campus. For schedule information, call (305) 871-1810.

www.greyhound.com

Miami Greyhound Bus Terminal
4111 NW 27th Street
Miami, FL 33142
(305) 871-1810

Amtrak

The Amtrak Train Station is near Hialeah, approximately eight miles from campus. For schedule information, visit http://amtrak.com/stations/mia.html

Miami Amtrak Train Station
8303 NW 37th Avenue
Miami, FL 33147
1-800-872-7245

Travel Agents

Worldwide Travel & Cruises
8784 SW 8th Street
Miami, (305) 223-2323

World Vacations Travel,
Suite 301
8725 NW 18th Terrace,
Miami, (305) 374-0774

Miami Travel
Suite 640
1200 Brickell Avenue
Miami, (305) 374-0550

Students Speak Out On...
Transportation

"There are many different options when it comes to transportation. We have a rail system that runs up and down Route 1 (the main highway on which the campus is located), which can be used to go to malls, shopping centers, and restaurants. There is also an on campus transportation system which transports students nightly to some of the surrounding hot spots."

Q "I have never used public transportation, except the Metrorail to games, but I know it's everywhere, and I know people who have used it daily and they say it's good."

Q "Transportation is not bad at all. I would recommend having a car so that you do not have to depend on someone else to take you from place to place. If not, you can always take the Hurry 'Cane. The Hurry 'Cane is a shuttle service provided free of charge to UM students. The shuttle goes all around campus, Publix, and Coconut Grove on the weekends. **Transportation is really very manageable here at the University of Miami**."

Q "**The Metrorail is right across the street,** and that can take you around town. It is not necessarily something you should ride on alone though."

Q "**The school offers its own transportation services** to get students around to the more popular spots. Cabs are always available, and the city of Miami's Metrorail is right across the street from campus. This can basically get you anywhere you need to go."

Q "Public transportation is very convenient with the Metrorail located directly across the street from campus. Aside from that, **school shuttles will take you to a lot of places on weekends,** or you can just catch a cab."

Q "**Public transportation is not as good as in somewhere like New York,** but I see taxis around campus a lot, so people must be using them. There's also the Metrorail, which most people use to go to the football games and I assume other places."

Q "**Miami has very good public transportation.** You can take the Metrorail and the Metromover all around the Miami area. You can also take the Tri-Rail all the way up to West Palm."

The College Prowler Take On...
Transportation

The lack of efficient public transportation in Miami can't really be blamed on any specific thing. For one, Miami isn't set up like New York or Chicago, cities whose metropolitan designs make it more convenient for trains and buses to get around. Since we're all living on heavily-paved swamp land down here, nothing can really be built underground. There are a few semblances of public transportation, notably the Metrorail, an elevated train system that gets little use anymore. The train runs along one line and makes stops at vital locations such as random office buildings, a Best Buy, the now empty Miami Arena, and, of course, the University of Miami. Some sketchy Miami citizens appear to actually use the Metrorail, but with no connecting cross trains it's mostly useless to students since Miami is, in fact, more than 20 feet wide.

The only traffic the Metrorail sees at its UM stop is on the days when the football team plays. The Orange Bowl is located off campus, so students get free access to the Metrorail on game days. But even then, buses have to meet them at a station closer to the stadium. No one really complains about the lack of public transportation, instead focusing their time on borrowing or stealing their friends' cars, or taking a free UM shuttle cleverly referred to as the Hurry 'Cane. Cabs aren't really widespread in Miami, but there are enough to get you home after a night of drinking or to take you to the airport, although most students prefer the cheaper Super Shuttle. UM does its part to make transportation easier for students without cars, offering free shuttles to grocery stores, shops, and movie theaters, as well as to various buildings around campus.

The College Prowler™ Grade on

Transportation: B

A high grade for Transportation indicates that campus buses, public buses, cabs, and rental cars are readily-available and affordable. Other determining factors include proximity to an airport and the necessity of transportation.

Weather

The Lowdown On...
Weather

Average Temperature		Average Precipitation	
Fall:	78 °F	Fall:	6.00 in.
Winter:	69 °F	Winter:	2.04 in.
Spring:	76 °F	Spring:	3.81 in.
Summer:	83 °F	Summer:	7.65 in.

Students Speak Out On...
Weather

"The weather is amazing, and is one of the reasons I chose this school in the first place. The temperature rarely ever goes below 55 degrees, so it is typically summer all year round. It is very rainy, however, in the spring, summer, and fall. The majority of clothing should probably be short sleeve shirts and shorts for guys, skirts or the like for girls, with just a couple other types of clothing for the rare colder weather."

Q "I brought t-shirts and flip flops when I first came, thinking Jimmy Buffet USA, but I was wrong. You don't need winter clothes, but you need a sweater and a rain jacket, and you will be fine. **The weather's amazing all year except the summer, but that's true anywhere**."

Q "**The weather is always hot!** In the winter it gets into the 50's and in the fall and spring it gets into the 80's and 90's. I recommend bringing plenty of shorts, jeans, t-shirts, collared shirts, a few sweaters, sandals, sneakers, and nice shoes with you to school. Also, bring one nice set of clothes to wear to a fancy restaurant or party. You do not need to bring any type of winter jacket, scarf, or snow hat. It's Florida!"

Q "**The weather is beautiful here.** Summer and spring all year round is one of the best parts of being in Miami. Bring your bathing suit and some sunglasses and you'll be ready for Miami."

Q "In December and January, the average temperature is low-to-mid 70's. That should say enough. **Bring a lot of warm-weather clothing**, and just a little cold-weather (it does occasionally dip down into the 40's and 50's, for a few hours at night)."

Q "**The weather is warm enough to wear shorts and a t-shirt 90% of the time** you're here. However, you get used to that, so when the temperature drops to the low 60's, and at its very lowest upper 40's, you freeze to death. So, bring some warm clothes for those days."

Q "**The weather is great almost all year round.** T-shirts are great, but the occasional sweater is helpful late in the fall semester and early in spring semester."

Q "**The weather is amazing,** especially after seeing the weather in other places during the winter. Bring sweatshirts for when you're inside because that's about as cold as it ever gets."

Q "Unless you are from South Florida, **you will find Miami to be hot**."

The College Prowler Take On...
Weather

Bring lots of heavy coats and sweatpants. You won't wear them, but you can always sell them on eBay for extra spending money during the semester. The unofficial University of Miami uniform for guys is basically cargo shorts, sandals, a hat or visor, and a t-shirt from an overrated band or beer company. Girls' tastes are of course more eclectic, but a typical wardrobe would be made up mostly of jeans, shorts, tank tops, and t-shirts, along with a few nice outfits for going out at night. Most students also suggest bringing umbrellas and rain ponchos, but you'll probably forget these in your room most of the time anyway.

The weather in Miami is beautiful throughout most of the year, but as soon as it dips below 70, people bring out the hooded sweatshirts and jeans. Students who grew up with snow and hail are reduced to shivering in between sips of steaming hot coffee after living in Miami for only a few months. But even on the coldest days of the year, when the temperature might drop into the high 40's, students refuse to lose the sandals, as if they're taking some kind of stand against the bitter cold. The biggest negative about Miami's weather is the chance for hurricanes every year. Despite recent watches and warnings, Miami has sustained little damage. Still, there are always threats of hurricanes every season. This could be a good thing, since sometimes school is canceled for hurricane warnings. But if a bad storm ever scores a direct hit on UM, some serious damage could be done, especially since some of the dorms have their outside walls composed entirely of glass. In daily life, the only problems with the weather are the unpredictable rain and the stifling heat in the summer, when most students go home anyway.

The College Prowler™ Grade on
Weather: A

A high Weather grade designates that temperatures are mild and rarely reach extremes, that the campus tends to be sunny rather than rainy, and that weather is fairly consistent rather than unpredictable.

Report Card Summary

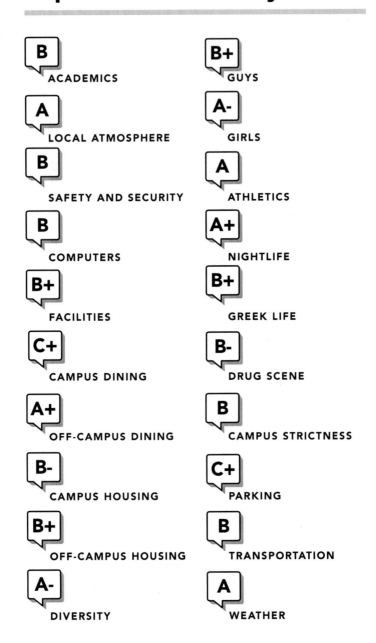

B ACADEMICS

A LOCAL ATMOSPHERE

B SAFETY AND SECURITY

B COMPUTERS

B+ FACILITIES

C+ CAMPUS DINING

A+ OFF-CAMPUS DINING

B- CAMPUS HOUSING

B+ OFF-CAMPUS HOUSING

A- DIVERSITY

B+ GUYS

A- GIRLS

A ATHLETICS

A+ NIGHTLIFE

B+ GREEK LIFE

B- DRUG SCENE

B CAMPUS STRICTNESS

C+ PARKING

B TRANSPORTATION

A WEATHER

Overall Experience

Students Speak Out On...
Overall Experience

{ **"I love it here, there is no place on earth I'd rather be getting my education. The only thing I gripe about is physics, but hey, we all have issues! Overall I'd give the school 4.5 stars out of 5"**

◯ "I love the University of Miami and have recommended it to many of my friends. I have enjoyed meeting new people and the Miami lifestyle. Never could I imagine myself anywhere but here."

◯ "I really like this school a lot. There are times when I wish I was back with my friends at home and sometimes I think that the girls are looking for the perfect hard body, which really sucks. But I have plenty of friends and the school is great."

Q "When you find the right situation, everything works out great. I **strongly suggest people come and enjoy everything this city has to offer**, and also the amazing experience that is Miami."

Q "**I enjoy this school immensely**, and have no regrets about coming here."

Q "**I made the best choice of my life choosing Miami** and I have no regrets. My overall experience has been so positive, words can't describe it. The friends I've made, the learning I've done, and the culture I've become accustomed to have made me much closer to the person I strive to be."

Q "This school suits me just fine. **I love it here.**"

Q "Overall, UM is okay. **I am not really happy with how much I pay to go to this place.** Sometimes I wish I was somewhere else when I consider the money that I pay, but otherwise it's a great school"

The College Prowler Take On...
Overall Experience

Despite daily griping about tuition costs, parking, thunderstorms, and hard classes, most students really seem to enjoy UM. Excellent attributes like the nightlife, weather, and culture seem to cancel out some of the bad things about being in Miami. For some students, these bad things include the unapproachable "hot" girls and guys on campus, while others find life in the dorms to be a challenge. The complaints about college are basically what you'd expect to hear anywhere. It appears that the bad things at UM really aren't that bad, but the good things are very good. Miami is one of the coolest cities in the world for a college student, and that goes deeper than just the superficial bar and club scene.

Students who are unhappy generally figure it out within a semester and transfer out of UM, usually to somewhere closer to home. But these are probably the type of people who would have been unhappy anywhere. College is tough, especially the first couple weeks if you come without knowing anyone. Making a whole new group of friends for the first time since kindergarten is one of the hardest and most stressful things you may ever have to do. But the end result of this process is friendships that you'll likely maintain for the rest of your life. Whether it's your roommate, classmates, fraternity brother, or sorority sister, college is a time when you should make friends and have fun. Despite the initial challenges of coming to college, there are few cities in the world that are as fun as Miami.

The Inside
Scoop

The Lowdown On...
The Inside Scoop

UM Slang

Know the slang, know the school. The following is a list of things you really need to know before coming to UM. The more of these words you know, the better off you'll be.

8-Care: Dial this on your room phone whenever the power goes out, the air conditioning breaks, or anything else goes wrong with school equipment, and a UM employee will come fix it.

Book Horizons: The sketchy bookstore across the street from campus that sometimes gets books cheaper than its on-campus rival. Also carries school supplies and UM merchandise.

Chartwells: The name of the two dining halls on campus. Also known to disgruntled students as Chart-Hells.

Dining Dollars: Money that comes with a student's meal plan, which can be used like a credit card at most of the restaurants on campus.

Easy: The name of the computer network where students can log in to retrieve their grades, professor rankings, course schedules, and most other student-related information.

Hurricane Drive: The street that runs through campus, past the baseball field and the fraternity houses. Connects Ponce to the back roads of the campus. Also known as San Amaro Drive.

Memorial: A long building that holds hundreds of classes per day, as well as the campus movie theater.

Metrorail: Miami's elevated train system that most students use only to get to the Orange Bowl on the days of football games.

Ponce: The smaller road running right past campus, which runs through downtown Coral Gables. Real name: Ponce de Leon Blvd.

Resident Master: A member of the faculty who lives in an apartment in the lobby of every residential college. The teacher and his or her family act as a host for the students living in the building and often have students over for dinner or meetings.

Sebastian the Ibis: The school's mascot, a common face around campus. The ibis is supposedly the last bird to leave before a hurricane and the first to return afterwards.

Stanford Circle: The driveway outside the UC where students get picked up and dropped off. The name refers to Stanford Drive, which is the main entrance to the campus.

The C-Store: The convenience store located in the UC, which stays open until the middle of the night and accepts dining dollars.

The IM Field: A giant field that is used for intramurals or just for fun. Has lights for night games.

The Lake: Lake Osceola, a huge body of water in the center of campus. A path around it connects the Towers to Eaton Residential College, the UC, and several campus buildings.

The LC: The Whitten Learning Center, a group of lecture-sized classrooms where many large classes are held.

The Pit: A large, mysterious hole in the ground behind Memorial where students study and hang out under the cover of thick trees.

The Rat: Refers to The Rathskellar, a popular bar on campus.

The Rock: The main area outside of the UC where pep rallies, protests, and other campus events are held.

The Towers: The dorms where most freshmen live, also known as Hecht and Stanford. There are actually two 12-story buildings in each dorm, making for four identical "towers" on one side of the lake.

The UC: The University Center, aptly located in the center of campus, which is home to the food court, a student lounge, the book store, a swimming pool, and assorted offices.

U.S. 1: The main road running near campus that is almost always insanely crowded. This road runs from Key West up to Maine, where the traffic must ease up slightly.

Unicco: The janitorial service on campus that cleans the floor bathrooms, halls, and study lounges. Treat the Unicco staff nicely or they may not get to your floor's bathroom for a while.

Things I Wish I Knew Before Coming to UM

• Get the smallest meal plan allowed.

• Make friends with people in your orientation group, especially ones of the opposite sex.

• Never buy school merchandise (clothes, hats, etc.) from the bookstore on campus, unless you like long lines and inflated prices.

• Leave your door open for the first week so people on the floor feel like they can talk to you. Walk around to others' rooms and talk to them.

• An up-to-date video game system will make you plenty of friends in a hurry.

• If you're a light sleeper, bring earplugs, because the freshman dorms are usually pretty loud late into the night.

• Bring a long Ethernet cord so you can use your laptop in bed.

• The air conditioners don't always do what you want, so be prepared to make wardrobe or linen adjustments.

• Bring plenty of quarters to wash clothes, because, for some reason, there are no change machines in the laundry rooms.

• Don't buy the posters they sell on campus in the first couple weeks. Prices plummet later in the semester when they're desperate to get rid of inventory.

Tips to Succeed at UM

- Talk to your professors. This is the number-one piece of advice

- Enjoy your major or you'll hate it here.

- Look up student evaluations of professors before you choose your classes.

- Sit in the front of the class and make sure the professor knows your name if you actually want to get something out of the course.

- Find people on your floor that have the same classes or major as you and share notes.

- Pick an academic adviser early and make sure he or she knows who you are and what your interests are.

- Pay attention to your advisers during orientation, especially when they talk about student life.

- Don't get too involved in campus activities unless you're confident in your grades and ability to study.

- Get used to using a computer for everything. There are plenty of classes that are very research-based, and hand-written assignments are rarely accepted anymore.

UM Urban Legends

- A lone crocodile makes its home in the lake on campus, where it sometimes feeds on fish in front of awed students. There are also rumors that the crocodile was removed by wildlife officials.
- A student drowned in the lake a couple years ago after taking a swim during a hurricane.
- Football players and other athletes go to the dining halls for steaks and huge portions of food not available to regular students.
- To the delight of the male student body, the Olsen twins were considering UM before settling on another school.

School Spirit

A popular chant at football games says, "It's great to be a Miami Hurricane!" Most students seem to feel this way, with plenty of school-related things to be proud of. The sports teams, notably football and baseball, are always among the top in the nation. The weather is great, the people are gorgeous, and the campus is beautiful. Shirts or hats with the school logo or colors on them are fairly common, as are cool little items like UM slippers, car magnets, and school supplies. Since UM is the only major college in the area, there is no direct rival other than schools from Central or Northern Florida like UF or FSU. Sporting events against these opponents attract huge crowds, while games against less-known opponents like Rutgers might have students sleeping in or heading to the beach instead.

Traditions

Homecoming is not an event exclusive to UM, but some of the events happening during the week are pretty unique. For example, the school always gets an old car and writes the name of the team we play in football that weekend. Students then line up to take out their aggression on the car, sledgehammer-style.

Iron Arrow is the university's oldest and most mysterious tradition. The true inner workings of this honor society are only available to its members, who are hand picked every semester. Membership is extremely limited and competitive, but members swear that this Seminole Indian-influenced organization has changed who they are.

The Breezeway is a tunnel that splits the UC in half, and is the site of a frenzied stockmarket-like atmosphere on weekday afternoons. The short, narrow walkway is full of students coming to and from classes, and so organizations set up tables to try to sell stuff or promote themselves. This can be a good thing if you're looking for weird antiques or girl scout cookies, and it does allow for some groups to get their name out, but overall it seems like a nuisance to most students.

Sportsfest is a yearly competition where residential colleges battle one another in various sporting events. The dorms, broken up by floor, field teams to compete in games ranging from football to rock, paper, scissors. The winner is declared Sportsfest champion and gets a trophy on display in the Wellness Center.

Hurricanes Help the Hometown is one of many service-oriented events taking place every year. For this, students dedicate a Saturday morning and afternoon to volunteering at dozens of locations all through Miami. Many of the participants are there from fraternities and sororities, since the event is part of Homecoming, but others come out just to help the community in any way they can.

Finding a Job or Internship

The Lowdown On...
Finding a Job or Internship

The Toppel Career Center is a great resource for students thinking ahead. There are numerous conventions on campus every year where hundreds of potential employers come to collect resumes or talk to students about job opportunities. As far as internships go, most individual schools within the university have a staff member to talk to students about internships during their stay at UM.

Advice

Get to know your school's internship adviser so that he or she comes to you first with the best offers. If you're looking to get started on internships early, talk to older students in your major to see if they can recommend something for you. Later on in your college career, head over to the Toppel Career Center and meet with someone there to discuss future job offers.

Career Center Resources & Services

- CaneTRAK

- Discover

- Vault

- Career Column

- Toppel Career Library

- Power Networking

- Career Exploration Week

- Career Development Series

Percent of Graduates Who Enter Job Market Within 6 Months After Graduation:

60%

Alumni

The Lowdown On...
Alumni

Website:
www.miami.edu/alumni

Office:
Office of Alumni Relations
1550 Brescia Avenue
Coral Gables, FL 33124
alumni@miami.edu
(305) 284-2872

Services Available

Entry to UM facilities like the library and Wellness Center, access to tickets for UM sporting events, a campus parking pass, and transcript services for members of the Alumni Association.

Major Alumni Events

Major alumni events include Homecoming, the Alumni Association Awards Program, class reunions, football games, and the Alumni Golf Tour. Alumni who choose to join the University of Miami Alumni Association are offered benefits including an Alumni ID card, access to university facilities, and inclusion in alumni websites and events.

Alumni Publications

Miami Magazine
Miami Magazine is published every semester and is included as a benefit of joining the University of Miami Alumni Association, which requires an annual contribution to maintain membership.

Did You Know?
Famous UM Alums—

Rick Berry (Class of '65), basketball Hall-of-Fame member, Roy Black (Class of '70), Criminal Defense attorney who handled Marv Albert's case, Gloria Estefan (Class of '78), singer/entertainer, Roy Firestone (Class of '75), TV personality and former ESPN host, Sandy Freedman (Class of '65), first woman mayor of Tampa, FL, Jerry Herman (Class of '53), Emmy-nominated musician and composer, Bruce Hornsby (Class of '77), singer/musician, Patricia Ireland (Class of '75), former National Organization for Women (NOW) president, Dwayne Johnson (Class of '95), professional wrestler and actor, known as "The Rock", Suzy Kolber (Class of '86), sideline reporter for ESPN, Ray Liotta (Class of '77), Golden Globe-nominated actor and producer, Alfred O'Hara (Class of '54), former space shuttle launch director, Al Rosen (Class of '48), former president of the Houston Astros baseball team, Jon Secada (Class of '83), singer/entertainer, Sylvester Stallone (Class of '99), Academy Award-nominated writer/actor for "Rocky", Lari White (Class of '88), Country singer

Student Organizations

A Week for Life – educated the community about HIV/AIDS.

Ad Group – students interested in advertising.

Adrian Empire – Medieval Times appreciation group. http://www.adrianempire.org/

African Students Union - http://www.miami.edu/studorgs/asu/

Aikido Club - http://www.miami.edu/studorgs/aikido/

Alpha Epsilon Delta – pre-med honor society. http://www.aedmiami.org/

Alpha Eta Mu Beta – biomedical engineering honor society.

Alpha Kappa Psi – business club. http://www.umakpsi.com/

Alpha Mu Music Theory Club

Alternative Spring Break

American Association of Pre-Dental Students

American Institute of Aeronautics and Astronautics

American Institute of Architecture Students

American Medical Student Association, Premedical Chapter - http://www.amsa.go.to/

American Society of Civil Engineers

American Society of Mechanical Engineers - http://www.eng.miami.edu/~umasme/

Amnesty International – UM chapter of a group promoting human rights.

Animal Allies - http://www.miami.edu/studorgs/hha/

Anthropology Club

Architectural Engineering Institute

Asian American Students Association - http://www.miami.edu/studorgs/aasa/

Association for Computing Machinery - http://www.acm.miami.edu/

Association of Commuter Students - http://www.miami.edu/studorgs/acs/

Association of Cuban-American Engineers - http://coeds.eng.miami.edu/~umace/

Association of Greek Letter Organizations

Association of Officials and Event Specialists

Athletes in Action – looks at religion in sports. http://www.athletesinaction.org/

AWARE! – promotes awareness of AIDS.

BACCHUS – promotes responsible consumption of alcohol. http://www.miami.edu/studorgs/bacchus/

Badminton - http://www.miami.edu/wellness-clubs/badminton/

Baptist College Ministries - http://www.miami.edu/studorgs/bcm/

Best Buddies - http://www.miami.edu/studorgs/bestbuddies/

Beta Beta Beta – a group of students interested in natural science

Bioethics Society - http://www.miami.edu/studorgs/bioethics/

Biomedical Engineering Society - http://www.eng.miami.edu/~umbmes/

Black Filmmakers Association

Black Nursing Student Association

Bowling Club

Brothers Overcoming Negativity and Destruction

Campus Advent – allows students to meet others with an interest in the Seventh-day Adventist denomination.

Campus Colors – a magazine supporting diversity on campus.

Campus Crusade for Christ - http://www.godsquad.com/

Canes for Cancer Awareness

Canes Kids - http://www.wementor.org/

Caribbean Students Association - http://www.miami.edu/studorgs/coiso/

Catholics Students Association - http://www.saintaugustinechurch.org/

Chi Alpha Christian Fellowship - http://www.miami.edu/studorgs/chialpha/

Circle K International – provides experience in group participation.

Colombian Student Association

Committee on Student Organizations - http://www.miami.edu/coso/

Council of International Students and Organizations - http://www.miami.edu/studorgs/coiso/

Cricket Club

Criminal Justice Club

Dancing Ibis – salsa dancing club. http://groups.yahoo.com/group/universityofmiamisalsa/

Delta Sigma Pi – supports the study of business and commercial ethics.

Earth Alert

Elections Commission - http://www.miami.edu/student-activities/

Engineering Advisory Board - http://www.eng.miami.edu/~umeab/

Entrepreneurship Board – applies classroom business lessons to the real world.

Episcopal Students Organization

Equestrian Club - http://www.miami.edu/studorgs/umet/

Federacion de Estudiantes Cubanos – promotes awareness of Cuban culture.

Fencing Club

Filipino Student Association - http://www.miami.edu/studorgs/fsa/

Florida Collegiate Music Educators National Conference

French Club

Friendship Club of China - http://phyvax.ir.miami.edu:8001/fcc/index2.html

FunDay – helps plan a day of friendship between UM students and people with mental disabilities

Generation-X Entrepreneur Club

Geological and Environmental Outings

German Club

Golden Key International Honour Society - http://www.miami.edu/studorgs/golden-key/

Golf Club - http://www.miami.edu/wellness/club/

Habitat for Humanity

Haitian Students Organization

Hindu Students Council - http://www.miami.edu/studorgs/hsc/

Hip-Hop Club - http://www.umhiphopclub.com/

Hispanic Heritage Month Association

History Club

Homecoming Executive Committee - http://www.miami.edu/homecoming/

Honor Students' Association - http://hsa.go.to/

Hui Aloha – promotes awareness of Hawaiian culture.

Hurricane Productions – an entertainment-planning committee for campus events. http://www.miami.edu/hurricane-productions/

Ibis – students create and produce all aspects of the yearbook.

Indian Students Association - http://www.um-isa.org/

Inquiry: The Research Connection – encourages students' interests in research

Institute of Industrial Engineers - http://www.eng.miami.edu/~umiie/

InterFraternity Council - http://www.miami.edu/studorgs/ifc/

InterVarsity Christian Fellowship

Islamic Society

Italian Club - http://umitalianclub.tripod.com/

Jewish Student Organization

KAOS – allows students to choreograph and perform hip-hop dances.

Karate Club

Latin America Student Association

Latino Greek Council

Latter-Day Saints Student Association

LINK – promotes leadership through volunteer events. http://www.miami.edu/studorgs/link/

Marine Mammal Stranding Team – helps rescue stranded marine mammals.

Men's Soccer Club - http://www.miami.edu/wellness/club/

Microbiology and Immunology Club - http://www.miami.edu/studorgs/microbiology/

Minority Association of Pre-Health Students

Mortar Board National Honor Society

Music and Entertainment Industry Student Association - http://www.miami.edu/studorgs/meisa/

Muslim Students Organization - http://www.miami.edu/studorgs/mso/

National Association of Black Accountants - http://www.nabainc.org/pages/Home.jsp

National Broadcasting Society - http://www.miami.edu/studorgs/nbs/

National Pan-Hellenic Council – governs the historically African American fraternities and sororities

National Society of Black Engineers - http://www.eng.miami.edu/~umnsbe/

National Society of Collegiate Scholars

OASIS – promotes Arab culture and history

Omicron Delta Kappa – a society for outstanding leaders on campus. http://www.miami.edu/studorgs/odk/

Organization for Jamaican Unity - http://www.miami.edu/studorgs/oju/

Panhellenic Association – governs the historically white sororities

Phi Alpha Delta, Pre-Legal Society - http://www.miami.edu/studorgs/pad/

Phi Sigma Pi National Leadership Fraternity

Phi Sigma Tau – an honor society for philosophy students. http://www.miami.edu/phi/phisigmatau/

Philosophy Club - http://www.miami.edu/phi/phiclub/

Project Sunshine – volunteers to help sick children at Miami Children's Hospital. http://www.projectsunshine.org/

Promoting Health Awareness Through Education - http://www.miami.edu/wellness/club/

Psi Chi – organization for students of psychology. http://www.miami.edu/studorgs/psi-chi/

Public Relations Student Society of America

QuantUM Entertainment – promotes the creation of student-produced entertainment. http://www.gotoquantum.com/

Racquetball Club

Roller Hockey Club - http://www.miami.edu/wellness-clubs/roller_hockey/

Rowing Club

Rugby Club - http://www.miami.edu/wellness/club/

Sailing Hurricanes - http://www.miami.edu/wellness-clubs/sailing/

Scandinavian Student Association

School of Architecture Student Council

Scuba Club - http://www.miami.edu/wellness/club/

Self-Experiencing Through Volunteering and Altruism

Society for the Study of Religions and Cultures - http://www.miami.edu/studorgs/ssrc/

Society of Hispanic Professional Engineers - http://www.eng.miami.edu/~umshpe/

Society of Manufacturing Engineers

Society of Women Engineers - http://www.eng.miami.edu/~umswe/

Solutions – allows students and faculty to informally discuss issues

SpectrUM – supports the acceptance of the gay, lesbian, and bisexual community. http://www.miami.edu/studorgs/spectrum/

Sport and Recreational Interest Clubs Federation

Squash Club

Strictly Business Association

Student Activity Fee Allocation Committee - http://www.miami.edu/safac/

Student Government

Student Health Advisory Committee

Students for a Free Tibet

Students Together Ending Poverty

Surfrider Club

Swimming and Aquatics Club

Table Tennis Club

Tae Kwon Do Club - http://www.miami.edu/wellness-clubs/tae-kwondo/

Technology Management Association

Tennis Club

The Associate Members of Lambda Sigma Upsilon – a Latino fraternity promoting educational and social experiences. http://www.lsu79.org/index_shield.html

Trinidad and Tobago Cultural Association - http://www.math.miami.edu/~ttca/tt.html

Ultimate Frisbee Club

United Black Students - http://www.miami.edu/studorgs/ubs/

United Dominicans Association - http://www.miami.edu/studorgs/uda/

University of Miami American Red Cross

University of Miami Baseball Club

University of Miami Filmmakers Association

University of Miami Lacrosse Club

University of Miami Percussion Club

University of Miami Young Democrats

Virgin Islands Student Association

Volleyball Club - http://www.miami.edu/wellness-clubs/volleyball/

Wesley Foundation – promotes Christian leadership. http://www.miami.edu/wesley/

William R. Butler Inspiration Concert Choir

Women in Business

Women's Fastpitch Softball Club

Women's Resource Center Programming Board - http://www.miami.edu/womens-center/

Women's Soccer Club - http://www.miami.edu/wellness/club/

WVUM – campus radio station. http://www.wvum.org/

Yanxin Qigong Club – practices traditional Chinese meditation

Yellow Rose Society – promotes awareness of female issues. http://groups.msn.com/yellowrosesociety/_homepage

The Best & The Worst

The Ten **BEST** Things About UM:

1	Sports teams
2	Hot guys and girls
3	Local clubs and bars in Miami. Miami has great nightlife, and some bars and clubs don't close until 4 a.m.
4	Walking around in December in sandals.
5	Local culture (Little Havana, South Beach, etc.)
6	Great off-campus restaurants
7	Arranging classes so that you have Mondays, Wednesdays, and Fridays off.
8	Walking past a lake and palm trees on the way to class every day.
9	Diversity
10	Miami's 24-hour culture

The Ten **WORST** Things About UM:

1 The traffic everywhere in Miami

2 When tropical storms and hurricanes cause several straight days of rain

3 Parking availability close to the dorms

4 Dining halls

5 Dorms with shared bathrooms

6 Struggling to understand Spanish and Spanish accents around Miami

7 The packed Metrorail ride to the Orange Bowl on game days

8 Waiting in line to register for classes

9 Lack of things to do late at night on campus (besides the C-Store)

10 Lack of "available." guys and girls

Visiting Miami

The Lowdown On...
Visiting UM

Overnight Stays

While the school does not offer any overnight programs, it would be a great experience to spend a night in the dorms with a current UM student. Check with any friends you may have at UM to see if they'll let you stay for a night, or, as a last resort, contact your high school's guidance office about past students who have gone to UM and see if they can put you in touch with an especially friendly one.

Be careful when you come, though. Every night of the week isn't like Saturday, even in party-happy Miami. Likewise, a Monday night might be more boring than a Thursday.

Hotel Information

Hotels in Coral Gables:

The Biltmore Hotel
www.biltmorehotel.com
1200 Anastasia Avenue
Coral Gables, FL 33134
(305) 445-1926
Distance from Campus:
2.2 miles
Price Range: $139-$199
(ask for UM corporate rate)

Holiday Inn-University of Miami
www.holiday-inn.com
1350 South Dixie Highway
Coral Gables, FL 33146
(305) 667-5611
Distance from Campus:
Less than a mile
Price Range: $74-$99
(with UM discount code UMPS)

Hyatt Regency Coral Gables
coralgables.hyatt.com
50 Alhambra Plaza
Coral Gables, FL 33134
(305) 441-1234
Distance from Campus:
3.5 miles
Price Range: $240-$260

Omni Colonnade Hotel
www.omnihotels.com
180 Aragon Ave.
Coral Gables, FL 33134
(305) 441-2600
Distance from Campus:
3.5 miles
Price Range: $139-$169
(ask for UM corporate rate)

Coconut Grove Hotels:|

Sonesta Hotel & Suites
www.sonesta.com
2889 McFarlane Road
Coconut Grove, FL 33133
(305) 529-2828
Distance from Campus:
2.7 miles
Price Range: $109-$119
(with UM discount code 100 GCP)

The Ritz-Carlton
www.ritzcarlton.com
3300 Southwest 27th Avenue
Coconut Grove, FL 33133
(305) 644-4680
Distance from Campus:
3.7 miles
Price Range: $279-$509

Grand Bay Hotel
www.wyndham.com
2669 South Bayshore Drive
Coconut Grove, FL 33133
(305) 858-9600
Distance from Campus:

3.1 miles
Price Range: $145
(with UM discount code #244)

The Mutiny Hotel
www.mutinyhotel.com
2951 South Bayshore Drive
Coconut Grove, FL 33133
(305) 441-2100
Distance from Campus:
2.9 miles
Price Range: $110-$149
(ask for UM discount)

Grove Isle Club and Resort
www.groveisle.com
Four Grove Isle Drive
Coconut Grove, FL 33133
(305) 858-8300
Distance from Campus:
5.2 miles

Price Range: $169-$359

South Beach:

The Alexander
www.alexanderhotel.com
5225 Collins Avenue
Miami Beach, FL 33140
(305) 865-6500
Distance from Campus: 16.1
miles
Price Range: $189-$279
(ask for UM discount)

Delano
www.ianschragerhotels.com
1685 Collins Avenue
Miami Beach, FL 33139
(305) 672-2000
Price Range: $345-$1600

Radisson Deauville Resort
www.radisson.com
6701 Collins Avenue
Miami Beach, FL 33141
(305) 865-8511
Distance from Campus:
17.2 miles
Price Range: $99-$119
(ask for UM discount)

Royal Palm Crowne Plaza Resort
www.sixcontinentshotels.com
1545 Collins Avenue
Miami Beach, FL 33139
(305) 604-5700
Distance from Campus:
13.7 miles
Price Range: $190
(ask for UM discount)

Wyndham Miami Beach Resort
www.wyndham.com
4833 Collins Avenue
Miami Beach, FL 33140
(305) 532-3600
Distance from Campus:
3.7 miles
Price Range: $89-$159
(ask for UM discount)

South Miami:

Miami Marriott Dadeland
www.marriotthotels.com
9090 S Dadeland Blvd.
Miami, FL 33156
(305) 670-1036
Distance from Campus:
3.5 miles
Price Range: $99-$154

Kendall:

AmeriSuites
www.amerisuites.com
11520 SW 88th Street
Miami, FL 33176
(305) 279-8688
Distance from Campus:
8.1 miles
Price Range: $119

Radisson Kendall Hotel and Suites
www.radisson.com
9100 N Kendall Drive
Miami, FL 33176
(305) 279-7700
Distance from Campus:
5.0 miles
Price Range: $99-$149

Take a Campus Virtual Tour

Go to: www.miami.edu/interactive-tour/

To Schedule a Group Information Session or Interview:

Call (305) 284-4323 to confirm the availability of an information session or come to the Office of Undergraduate Admission on any weekday at 12:30 p.m.

Admissions officers hold information sessions at 12:30 p.m. every Monday-Friday at the Office of Undergraduate Admission on campus. This office is located in the Bowman Foster Ashe building. Check with the office at the number above to confirm that a session will be held on the day of your visit. Reservations are not required.

Campus Tours

Campus tours leave during the school year every week day at 11 a.m., 1:30 p.m., and 3 p.m. from the Office of Undergraduate Admission. Saturday tours are available by appointment during the school year and are not available during the summer. Weekday tours during the summer leave at 11 a.m. All tours last approximately one hour and are led by current UM students.

Directions to Campus

Driving from the North:
- Take I-95 south, until it ends and turns into U.S. 1.
- Take U.S. 1 south for about five miles and turn right onto Stanford Drive.
- Go straight on Stanford through the main gates of the school.

Driving from the South:
- Take U.S. 1 north and make a left onto Stanford Drive.
- Go straight on Stanford through the main gates of the school.

Driving from the East:
- Drive west until you reach U.S. 1 and follow the instructions above. (Not many people live east of UM)

Driving from the West:
- Take Miller Road east until it ends at San Amaro Drive and make a right.
- Take San Amaro Drive for about a half-mile until it ends and turn left onto Ponce De Leon Blvd. Take Ponce De Leon Blvd. for about a mile and turn left onto Stanford Drive into the main gates of the school.

Words to Know

Academic Probation – A student can receive this if they fail to keep up with their school's academic minimums. Those who are unable to improve their grades after receiving this warning can possibly face dismissal.

Beer Pong / Beirut – A drinking game with numerous cups of beer arranged in a particular pattern on each side of a table. The goal is to get a ping pong ball into one of the opponent's cups by throwing the ball or hitting it with a paddle. If the ball lands in a cup, the opponent is required to drink the beer.

Bid – An invitation from a fraternity or sorority to pledge their specific house.

Blue-Light Phone – Brightly-colored phone posts with a blue light bulb on top. These phones exist for security purposes and are located at various outside locations around most campuses. If a student has an emergency or is feeling endangered, they can pick up one of these phones (free of charge) to connect with campus police or an escort service.

Campus Police – Policemen who are specifically assigned to a given institution. Campus police are not regular city officers; they are employed by the university in a full-time capacity.

Club Sports – A level of sports that falls somewhere between varsity and intramural. If a student is unable to commit to a varsity team but has a lot of passion for athletics, a club sport could be a better, less intense option. If a club sport still requires too much commitment, intramurals often involve no traveling and a lot less time.

Cocaine – An illegal drug. Also known as "coke" or "blow," cocaine often resembles a white crystalline or powdery substance. It is highly addictive and dangerous.

Common Application – An application that students can use to apply to multiple schools.

Course Registration – The time when a student selects what courses they would like for the upcoming quarter or semester. Prior to registration, it is best to have an idea of several back-up courses in case a particular class becomes full. If a course is full, a student can place themselves on the waitlist, although this still does not guarantee entry.

Division Athletics – Athletics range from Division I to Division III. Division IA is the most competitive, while Division III is considered to be the least competitive.

Dorm – Short for dormitory, a dorm is an on-campus housing facility. Dorms can provide a range of options from suite-style rooms to more communal options that include shared bathrooms. Most first-year students live in dorms. Some upperclassmen who wish to stay on campus also choose this option.

Early Action – A way to apply to a school and get an early acceptance response without a binding commitment. This is a system that is becoming less and less available.

Early Decision – An option that students should use only if they are positive that a place is their dream school. If a student applies to a school using the early decision option and is admitted, they are required and bound to attend that university. Admission rates are usually higher with early decision students because the school knows that a student is making them their first choice.

Ecstasy – An illegal drug. Also known as "E" or "X," ecstasy looks like a pill and most resembles an aspirin. Considered a party drug, ecstasy is very dangerous and can be deadly.

Ethernet – An extremely fast internet connection that is usually available in most university-owned residence halls. To use an Ethernet connection properly, a student will need a network card and cable for their computer.

Fake ID – A counterfeit identification card that contains false information. Most commonly, students get fake IDs and change their birthdates so that they appear to be older than 21 (of legal drinking age). Even though it is illegal, many college students have fake IDs in hopes of purchasing alcohol or getting into bars.

Frosh – Slang for "freshmen."

Hazing – Initiation rituals that must be completed for membership into some fraternities or sororities. Numerous universities have outlawed hazing due to its degrading or dangerous requirements.

Sports (IMs) – A popular, and usually free, student activity where students create teams and compete against other groups for fun. These sports vary in competitiveness and can include a range of activities—everything from billiards to water polo. IM sports are a great way to meet people with similar interests.

Keg – Officially called a half barrel, a keg contains roughly 200 12-ounce servings of beer and is often found at college parties.

LSD – An illegal drug. Also known as acid, this hallucinogenic drug most commonly resembles a tab of paper.

Marijuana – An illegal drug. Also known as weed or pot; besides alcohol, marijuana is one of the most commonly-found drugs on campuses across the country.

Major –The focal point of a student's college studies; a specific topic that is studied for a degree. Examples of majors include physics, English, history, computer science, economics, business, and music. Many students decide on a specific major before arriving on campus, while others are simply "undecided" and figure it out later. Those who are extremely interested in two areas can also choose to double major.

Meal Block – The equivalent of one meal. Students on a "meal plan" usually receive a fixed number of meals per week.

Each meal, or "block," can be redeemed at the school's dining facilities in place of cash. More often than not, if a student fails to use their weekly allotment of meal blocks, they will be forfeited.

Minor – An additional focal point in a student's education. Often serving as a compliment or addition to a student's main area of focus, a minor has fewer requirements and prerequisites to fulfill than a major. Minors are not required for graduation from most schools; however some students who want to further explore many different interests choose to have both a major and a minor.

Mushrooms – An illegal drug. Also known as "shrooms," this drug looks like regular mushrooms but are extremely hallucinogenic.

Off-Campus Housing – Housing from a particular landlord or rental group that is not affiliated with the university. Depending on the college, off-campus housing can range from extremely popular to non-existent. Those students who choose to live off campus are typically given more freedom, but they also have to deal with things such as possible subletting scenarios, furniture, and bills. In addition to these factors, rental prices and distance often affect a student's decision to move off campus.

Office Hours – Time that teachers set aside for students who have questions about the coursework. Office hours are a good place for students to go over any problems and to show interest in the subject material.

Pledging – The time after a student has gone through rush, received a bid, and has chosen a particular fraternity or sorority they would like to join. Pledging usually lasts anywhere from one to two semesters. Once the pledging period is complete and a particular student has done everything that is required to become a member, they are considered a brother or sister. If a fraternity or a sorority would decide to "haze" a group of students, these initiation rituals would take place during the pledging period.

Private Institution – A school that does not use taxpayers dollars to help subsidize education costs. Private schools typically cost more than public schools and are usually smaller.

Prof – Slang for "professor."

Public Institution – A school that uses taxpayers dollars to help subsidize education costs. Public schools are often a good value for in-state residents and tend to be larger than most private colleges.

Quarter System (sometimes referred to as the Trimester System) – A type of academic calendar system. In this setup, students take classes for three academic periods. The first quarter usually starts in late September or early October and concludes right before Christmas. The second quarter usually starts around early to mid–January and finishes up around March or April. The last quarter, or "third quarter," usually starts in late March or early April and finishes up in late May or Mid-June. The fourth quarter is summer. The major difference between the quarter system and semester system is that students take more courses but with less coverage.

RA (Resident Assistant) – A student leader who is assigned to a particular floor in a dormitory in order to help to the other students who live there. A RA's duties include ensuring student safety and providing guidance or assistance wherever possible.

Recitation – An extension of a specific course; a "review" session of sorts. Because some classes are so large, recitations offer a setting with fewer students where students can ask questions and get help from professors or TAs in a more personalized environment. As a result, it is common for most large lecture classes to be supplemented with recitations.

Rolling Admissions – A form of admissions. Most commonly found at public institutions, schools with this type of policy continue to accept students throughout the year until their class sizes are met. For example, some schools begin accepting students as early as December and will continue to do so until April or May.

Room and Board – This is typically the combined cost of a university-owned room and a meal plan.

Room Draw/Housing Lottery – A common way to pick on-campus room assignments for the following year. If a student decides to remain in university-owned housing, they are assigned a unique number that, along with seniority, is used to choose their new rooms for the next year.

Rush – The period in which students can meet the brothers and sisters of a particular chapter and find out if a given fraternity or sorority is right for them. Rushing a fraternity or a sorority is not a requirement at any school. The goal of rush is to give students who are serious about pledging a feel for what to expect.

Semester System – The most common type of academic calendar system at college campuses. This setup typically includes two semesters in a given school year. The "fall" semester starts around the end of August or early September and finishes right before winter vacation. The "spring" semester usually starts in mid-January and ends around late April or May.

Student Center/Rec Center/Student Union – A common area on campus that often contains study areas, recreation facilities, and eateries. This building is often a good place to meet up with fellow students and is most commonly used as a hangout. Depending on the school, the student center can have a huge role or a non-existent role in campus life.

Student ID – A university-issued photo ID that serves as a student's key to many different functions within an institution. Some schools require students to show these cards in order to get into dorms, libraries, cafeterias, and other facilities. In addition to storing meal plan information, in some cases, a student ID can actually work as a debit card and allow students to purchase things from bookstores or local shops.

Suite – A type of dorm room. Unlike other places that have communal bathrooms that are shared by the entire floor, a suite has a private bathroom. Suite-style dorm rooms can house anywhere from two to ten students.

TA (Teacher's Assistant) – An undergraduate or grad student who helps in some manner with a specific course. In some cases, a TA will teach a class, assist a professor, grade assignments, or conduct office hours.

Undergraduate – A student who is in the process of studying for their Bachelor (college) degree.

ABOUT THE AUTHOR:

Writing this book has been one of the biggest projects I've ever undertaken. Maybe this is a tribute to just how extremely lazy I've been for the past 19 years, but I've never had to do something this big that required both heavy research and thinking objectively about a place that I love. In the process of writing this 30,000 word guide to the University of Miami, I realized some things about college life that I had never considered before.

At whatever college you end up attending, you will find things you like and things you hate. The College Prowler guidebooks are a terrific example of this. There are no colleges with straight A's, and none with straight F's. If there were perfect colleges out there, everyone would flock there, and if there were totally miserable schools, they'd be empty.

The trick to enjoying college is to find a place that excels in the areas that you find important. For me, nightlife is not as important as academics. Chances are, if you narrow down what you're looking for, there will be a few schools that are right for you. Making the final decision on where to go involves a ton of factors, but you should know that there isn't just one college in the world that will make you happy. Unless you make a terrible mistake, wherever you end up going is probably going to suit your needs. You will seek out the kind of people you want to be friends with, even if you don't mean to. Your senior year of high school is a great time to have fun, but it also involves the biggest decision you've ever had to make. The best advice I can give is to do research, visit campuses, talk to students, and follow your heart. If you end up hating it, just transfer.

Although I've found some of the details in this book to be a little excessive (Is anyone really basing their college decisions on the cost of a ticket for parking in a fire lane?), I feel privileged to have been given the chance to write it. In doing so, I feel like I've learned much more about myself and about the University of Miami and the city around it. It has been incredibly hard to write negative things about this place, because coming here was the best choice I've ever made. Still, I hope this book is fair and informative, and if you have any further questions or just want to talk to a student, I would love to get some E-mail at ShawnWines@collegeprowler.com that doesn't promote webcams and Viagra.

I'll close this out by saying thanks to the many people who've helped me complete this thing. Thanks to Julian, Sasha, Guy, Jacob, Matt, and Carey for finally getting those surveys back to me. It took you long enough. Special thanks to Rich for driving around with me and finding out the hours of all the local restaurants who refuse to answer questions over the phone. Thanks to Rosh and Anthony for your advice and comments on all those clubs I've never been to. Thanks to Mike for your knowledge about all the bars and for being a cool enough roommate to let me sit at my computer and write this thing for four weeks, even though I know my chair blocks your view of the TV. And of course, thanks to my parents and all of my family for their never ending love, support, advice, and friendship. Please send money.

Shawn Wines

Notes

....

....

....

....

....

....

....

....

....

....

....

....

....

....

Notes

....

....

....

....

....

....

....

....

....

....

....

....

....

Notes

Notes

....

....

....

....

....

....

....

....

....

....

....

....

....

Notes

....

....

....

....

....

....

....

....

....

....

....

....

....

Notes

....

....

....

....

....

....

....

....

....

....

....

....

....

Notes

....

....

....

....

....

....

....

....

....

....

....

....

....

Notes

....

....

....

....

....

....

....

....

....

....

....

....

....

Notes

Notes

Notes

Notes

....

....

....

....

....

....

....

....

....

....

....

....

....

Notes

....

....

....

....

....

....

....

....

....

....

....

....

....

Notes

....

....

....

....

....

....

....

....

....

....

....

....

....

Notes

....

....

....

....

....

....

....

....

....

....

....

....

....

....

Notes

....

....

....

....

....

....

....

....

....

....

....

....

....

Notes

....

....

....

....

....

....

....

....

....

....

....

....

....

Notes

....

....

....

....

....

....

....

....

....

....

....

....

....

Need More Help?

Do you have more questions about this school?
Can't find a certain statistic? College Prowler is
here to help. We are the best source of college
information on the planet. We have a network
of thousands of students who can get the latest
information on any school to you ASAP.
E-mail us at *info@collegeprowler.com* with your
college-related questions. It's like having an
older sibling show you the ropes!

Email Us Your College-Related Questions!

Check out **www.collegeprowler.com** for more details.
1.800.290.2682

Notes

....

....

....

....

....

....

....

....

....

....

....

....

....

Tell Us What Life Is Really Like At Your School!

Have you ever wanted to let people know what your school is really like? Now's your chance to help millions of high school students choose the right school.

Let your voice be heard and win cash and prizes!

Check out **www.collegeprowler.com** for more info!

Notes

....

....

....

....

....

....

....

....

....

....

....

....

....

Notes

....

....

....

....

....

....

....

....

....

....

....

....

....

Pros and Cons

Still can't figure out if this is the right school for you?
You've already read through this in-depth guide; why not
list the pros and cons? It will really help with narrowing down
your decision and determining whether or not
this school is right for you.

Pros	Cons

Notes

....

....

....

....

....

....

....

....

....

....

....

....

....

Notes

....

....

....

....

....

....

....

....

....

....

....

....

....

Notes

....

....

....

....

....

....

....

....

....

....

....

....

....

Do You Own A Website?

Would you like to be an affiliate of one of the fastest-growing companies in the publishing industry? Our web affiliates generate a significant income based on customers whom they refer to our website. Start making some cash now! Contact *sales@collegeprowler.com* for more information or call 1.800.290.2682

Apply now at **www.collegeprowler.com**

Notes

....

....

....

....

....

....

....

....

....

....

....

....

....

Reach A Market Of Over 24 Million People.

Advertising with College Prowler will provide you with an environment in which your message will be read and respected. Place your message in a College Prowler guidebook, and let us start bringing long-lasting customers to you. We deliver high-quality ads in color or black-and-white throughout our guidebooks.

Contact Joey Rahimi
joey@collegeprowler.com
412.697.1391
1.800.290.2682

Check out **www.collegeprowler.com** for more info.

Notes

....

....

....

....

....

....

....

....

....

....

....

....

....

Write For Us!
Get Published! Voice Your Opinion.

Writing a College Prowler guidebook is both fun and rewarding; our open-ended format allows your own creativity free reign. Our writers have been featured in national newspapers and have seen their names in bookstores across the country. Now is your chance to break into the publishing industry with one of the country's fastest-growing publishers!

Apply now at **www.collegeprowler.com**

Contact *editor@collegeprowler.com* or call 1.800.290.2682 for more details.

Notes

....

....

....

....

....

....

....

....

....

....

....

....

....